Kindness, Clarity, and Insight

Kindness, Clarity, & Insight

:   The Fourteenth Dalai Lama
:   His Holiness Tenzin Gyatso

Revised and Updated

Edited and translated by Jeffrey Hopkins
Co-edited by Elizabeth Napper

Snow Lion Publications

ITHACA, NEW YORK • BOULDER, COLORADO

Snow Lion Publications
P. O. Box 6483
Ithaca, NY 14851 USA
(607) 273-8519
www.snowlionpub.com

Printed in USA on acid-free recycled paper.

ISBN-10 1-55939-251-7
ISBN-13 978-1-55939-251-8

*The Library of Congress catalogued the previous edition
of this book as follows:*

Bstan-'dzin-rgya-mtsho, Dalai Lama XIV, 1935-
   Kindness, clarity, and insight / the Fourteenth Dalai Lama, his Holiness
Tenzin Gyatso ; translated and edited by Jeffrey Hopkins ; co-edited by
Elizabeth Napper.
     p. cm.
   ISBN 0-937938-18-1 (pbk.)
     1. Buddhism—Doctrines. 2. Buddhism—China—Tibet.
I. Hopkins, Jeffrey. II. Napper, Elizabeth.
BQ7935.B774K56 1984
294.3'4—dc19
                                                    84-51198

Designed and typeset by Gopa & Ted2, Inc

CONTENTS

PREFACE

. . .

NOW LION PUBLICATIONS, now celebrating its twenty-fifth year as the preeminent publisher of books exclusively on Tibet and Tibetan Buddhism, grew out of the wish to make available to the general public the profoundly appealing series of lectures that His Holiness the Dalai Lama gave in the United States in 1979 and 1981, and in Canada in 1980. Although the Dalai Lama had escaped from Tibet to India during a public demonstration against the Chinese Communist occupation in 1959, the U.S. government repeatedly had caved in to Chinese pressure and did not allow him to visit this country until the Carter Administration in 1979.

Prodded by Joel McCleary, deputy assistant to President Carter, and myself at a meeting in the White House with key staff from the National Security Council, the Carter Administration (which from its inception was concerned with human rights) undoubtedly saw the human rights issues involved, and agreed to permit the Dalai Lama's visit. Although they requested a six-month delay before the visit, this fit right in with our wishes, since extensive preparations had to be made by the Office of Tibet in New York under the leadership of Tenzin Tethong (later to become Prime Minister of the exiled Tibetan government headquartered in Dharamsala, India) for what became a forty-nine day, twenty-four city lecture tour with sixty-seven talks. The first planning meeting between McCleary, Tenzin Tethong, and myself began in McCleary's office in the Executive Office Building several days after the meeting at which approval was given for the trip, and continued through lunch in the restaurant under the Oval Office in the White House. McCleary and Deputy Assistant to the President Tom Beard were particularly effective in overcoming many bureaucratic obstacles to the Dalai Lama's final visa approval, making Washington contacts with future friends and allies of His Holiness such as Congressman Charlie Rose, and arranging for security throughout the trip for the then relatively unknown Dalai Lama.

Tenzin Tethong formed a committee to arrange the details of the visit, which focused on the content of the lectures and avoided any media hype. This meant that His Holiness' introduction to the U.S. was on the basis of his message of compassion, meditative concentration, and examination of reality, leading to the title of the collection of his talks in this book, *Kindness, Clarity, and Insight.*

Broad in scope and revealing the depths of his knowledge, the lectures moved from the East Coast to the South, the Midwest, the West Coast, the Upper Midwest, and again the East Coast. These teachings introduced the range of the Dalai Lama and his message in a dynamic and concise way to the English-speaking world, covering a plethora of topics—the need for compassion in society and the world, the cause and effect of karma, the four noble truths, the luminous nature of the mind, the common goals of the world's religions, meditative concentration, emptiness and selflessness, the two truths, and the fundamental innate mind of clear light that all the various schools of Tibetan Buddhism aim at manifesting. Although others in Tibet have mentioned that all orders of Tibetan Buddhism have the same basic outlook, His Holiness has been the first to explain in detail how this is so, his brilliant syncretic exposition being the final chapter in this book.

In 1979 the only books by the Dalai Lama in English, or any other language except Tibetan, were his autobiography, *My Land and My People,* and *The Buddhism of Tibet and the Key to the Middle Way.* In Ithaca, New York, and later in Toronto, the young, idealistic, compassionately motivated but nearly penniless founders of Snow Lion Publication approached His Holiness for counsel on how to communicate the breadth and depth of Tibetan Buddhism to the English-speaking world. The Dalai Lama quickly expressed his enthusiasm for a publishing house that could serve two audiences. In his own words (recorded during that audience):

> Basically, two main types of books are needed: one chiefly for study by scholars and academically minded practitioners and another primarily for practitioners without much concern for deeper philosophy. These two basic types are essentially the same, but have slightly different approaches. One is more detailed, while the other is more condensed. If you can make both of these available, that would be excellent.

Snow Lion has brilliantly succeeded in both of these avenues, providing a massive, diverse body of texts for an ever-growing audience throughout the world where interest in Tibetan Buddhism has spread. Although many publishing houses have produced books on Tibet and Tibetan Buddhism, Snow Lion has remained, through thick and thin, the only one publishing exclusively in this area, keeping almost all of its back list of over two hundred titles in print throughout these twenty-five years. Thus, the apparent leap of confidence in permitting this unknown, underfunded, inexperienced company to publish this important first book of his teachings in the West has borne rich fruit.

In addition, His Holiness counseled the founders of Snow Lion to be nonsectarian and unbiased in their efforts and to publish what is of value from all schools of Tibetan Buddhism and from Bön, the pre-Buddhist religion of Tibet. Following His Holiness' advice, Snow Lion has been remarkably successful in becoming a platform for all of Tibet's great spiritual traditions.

It all began with this book, *Kindness, Clarity, and Insight,* the first book of teachings by the Dalai Lama in the English-speaking world. Foundational to His Holiness' message, it is now reissued in this celebratory twenty-fifth year. With this book serving as a model, scores of writers have been inspired to turn his oral teachings into books; it is likely that the Dalai Lama has inspired more writers to work with him on publications than any other person in the world, these mutual efforts now totaling more than sixty books.

Kindness, Clarity, and Insight draws on his lecture tours in the United States in 1979 and 1981, and in Canada in 1980. The Dalai Lama spoke at scores of universities, colleges, ecumenical gatherings, Buddhist centers, and public meetings, gradually explaining his message of the need for kindness, compassion, concentration, and penetrative insight in the world. Serving as interpreter, I was continually amazed and moved at the personal relevance of his message, its practicality and applicability, for as he says, human society begins with people and specifically our capacity to recognize in others our common aspirations to happiness. The appeal is to the heart by way of the mind, using reason and sense to curb selfishness and to generate deeply felt altruism based on wisdom.

Although the teachings in this book are the result of just the first three trips of the Dalai Lama in North America, they comprehend and encapsulate in a concise and crisp manner all of the topics to which he has returned repeatedly, and eloquently, in his subsequent speaking tours—the core subject matter of Tibetan Buddhism. Readers of this single volume, undaunting in size, will be well prepared for understanding all of the Dalai Lama's subsequent books. Translated into twelve languages, including Tibetan, the book remains the heart-message of this great world leader.

The book contains presentations of basic Buddhist doctrines—how to develop clarity of mind useful in all walks of life and how to penetrate beyond appearances to the profound nature of both persons and other phenomena, thereby negotiating the conflict between appearance and reality. His is a message of hope, both in terms of the potential for individual and social transformation and in terms of the potential of the human spirit.

Centering around fundamental Buddhist attitudes that are at the core of His Holiness the Dalai Lama's outlook, the twenty chapters are deliberately arranged in a developmental sequence so as to allow the reader to acquire the necessary background to appreciate the more complex, later topics.[1] Thus, the teachings in this book, taken as a whole, provide a map of Tibetan spiritual culture.

THE POLITICAL SITUATION

The Dalai Lama has directed the rebuilding of Tibetan cultural institutions outside of Tibet in India and Nepal. Also, asking religious and political leaders of the world to look beyond narrow interests to the greater good, he has advocated attention to the fundamental need of society regardless of religion or politics—kindness. But when the Chinese Communist government in Beijing hears that the Dalai Lama has been invited to visit a country, it immediately objects to that government, which sometimes then finds his visit to be inconvenient, or downscales the visit, or makes it "personal." What do they fear? The Dalai Lama has no army, no economic pressure, no political cards to play. He advocates nonviolence and compassion.

In 1978, the Chinese Communist government in Beijing offered to negotiate anywhere at anytime if the Dalai Lama would not bring up the topic of independence. He agreed to this condition, but the response for now almost three decades has been to refuse to engage in substantive talks. What do they fear?

His power comes from a life of ethics, the force of truth. In Tibetan, he speaks with a range, depth, inspiration, humor, and sincerity that inspire insight and motivate dedication to others' welfare. I have often wished that all the world could hear this marvel in his own tongue.

His full name is *rJe btsun 'jam dpal ngag dbang blo bzang ye shes bstan 'dzin rgya mtsho srid gsum dbang bsgyur mtshungs pa med pa'i sde dpal bzang po,* which in English, syllable-by-syllable, is "Leader-Holiness-Gentleness-Renown-Speech-Dominion-Mind-Goodness-Primordial-Wisdom-Teaching-Hold-Vastness-Ocean-Being-Triad-Controlling-Unparalleled-Glory-Integrity." Many years ago, I wrote a poem around his name which I would like to share with you:

Leader of the world recognized for true **holiness**,
Gentleness personified in persuasive **renown**,
Speech of compassion pervading the planet in its **dominion**,
Mind of altruistic endeavor reaching all in its **goodness**,
Primordial in the depth and range of profound **wisdom**,
Teaching encompassing all phenomena in its **hold**,
Vastness of love's deeds rippling throughout life's **ocean**,
Being so merciful displayed in suffering's **triad**,
Controlling the unruly through kindness **unparalleled**,
Glory in forms of endeavor sealed in total **integrity**,
May the teacher of the world, bearing compassion
And wisdom indissoluble, see all obstacles dissolve.

Jeffrey Hopkins
Professor Emeritus of Tibetan Studies
University of Virginia

EDITORS' NOTE

. . .

OCCASIONAL FOOTNOTES have been provided by the editors giving brief explanations, references to supplementary material, and references for quotations, the latter kindly located in the Tibetan by Kensur Yeshe Thupten. In rendering Sanskrit words in the body of the text, ch, sh, and ṣh are used in place of c, ś, and ṣ for the sake of easy pronunciation. Transliteration of Tibetan is done in accordance with a system devised by Turrell Wylie (see "A Standard System of Tibetan Transcription," *Harvard Journal of Asiatic Studies* 22 (1959):261–267).

RELIGIOUS VALUES
AND HUMAN SOCIETY

. . .

CONSTITUTION HALL, WASHINGTON, D.C.

INTRODUCTION BY
CONGRESSMAN CHARLES G. ROSE

THIS IS A HOLY INSTANT for all Americans. Speaking on behalf on my colleagues in Congress who are joining to welcome His Holiness to Capitol Hill tomorrow I want to thank you for coming tonight to Constitution Hall. I thank you because the United States Government is enriched by this visit.

I have read about the Buddhist concepts of karma and dharma. I even reviewed the 227 rules that Buddhist monks must follow, and then I realized how much I have to learn. But I came to the conclusion that what it is all about is self-awareness. Enlightenment starts within the individual. And if America is to cope with its current dilemmas, it must reach a higher level of consciousness than the level at which our problems were created. The belief of Tibetan Buddhism in the evolution of the individual is harmonious with the desire of a growing number of our citizens for spiritual growth to reach a higher consciousness. People involved with spiritual belief too often renounce politics and ordinary life. What His Holiness teaches is that one aspect of life connects with every other. Political solutions are linked directly with spiritual growth, and that is why this visit is so timely for America. The message of Tibetan Buddhism is entirely consistent with our Jewish and Christian heritage. The visionary humanism of His Holiness may even help us to find a more authentic expression of the religions with which we are familiar. All the world's religions lead along the same path.

This visit comes appropriately within a month of the arrival of another great spiritual leader, His Holiness, the Pope of the Roman Catholic faith. We in Washington are grateful to receive these visits and to heed the insights of those conversant with this wisdom, a wisdom to which politicians aspire but seldom achieve. The Dalai Lama encourages people to think more for themselves, and that is essential for our nation and our world. His Holiness has nourished the seed of Buddhism which is growing in the United States, but America's reverence for such ideals is not new. The American poet Henry Thoreau spoke of love of Jesus Christ and love of the Buddha, but said that love was the main thing.

Our nation has been involved in the tragic wars of Asia. But the time has now come when we are well-advised to involve ourselves in a better understanding of the great peaceful teachings of Asia such as Tibetan Buddhism, and let us seek paths of love and consciousness and personal transformation. His Holiness is a guide to enlightenment; we respect his quiet strength, a spiritual power that cannot be suppressed even if lands are occupied and temples are closed and prayers are suppressed. History has taught that oppression is transformed by faith and that oppressors eventually get what they resist.

We meet in this hall which honors the Constitution of the United States. I remind you of the first amendment to the Constitution which states that the "Congress shall make no law respecting an establishment of religion, or prohibiting the free exercise thereof." Tonight we celebrate the free exercise of religion, in this instance, the Buddhism of Tibet, in this historic hall. We do so by welcoming the distinguished spiritual and temporal leader of Tibet, His Holiness the Dalai Lama. It is my great honor to introduce to this group of his friends and followers His Holiness.

His Holiness the Dalai Lama's Talk

IN ONE WAY—in material terms—this present generation has reached a high level of development. Yet at the same time, we human beings are facing many problems. Some are due to external events or causes, such as natural disasters. These we cannot avoid. However, many problems are created by our own mental defects; we suffer due to an internal lack. I call these problems unnecessary ones, for if we adopt a right mental attitude, these man-made problems need not arise.

Often they are due to differences in ideology, and unfortunately different religious faiths are also sometimes involved. Hence it is very important that we have a right attitude. There are many different philosophies, but what is of basic importance is compassion, love for others, concern for others' suffering, and reduction of selfishness. I feel that compassionate thought is the most precious thing there is. It is something that only we human beings can develop. And if we have a good heart, a warm heart, warm feelings, we will be happy and satisfied ourselves, and our friends will experience a friendly and peaceful atmosphere as well. This can be experienced nation to nation, country to country, continent to continent.

The basic principle is compassion, love for others. Underlying all is the valid feeling of "I," and on a conventional level there is an "I"— "I want this," "I do not want that." We experience this feeling naturally, and naturally we want happiness—"I want happiness," "I do not want suffering." Not only is it natural, it is right. It needs no further justification; it is a natural feeling validated simply by the fact that we naturally and correctly want happiness and do not want suffering.

Based on that feeling, we have the right to obtain happiness and the right to get rid of suffering. Further, just as I myself have this feeling and this right, so others equally have the same feeling and the same right. The difference is that when you say "I," you are speaking of just one single person, one soul. Others are limitless. Thus, you should visualize the following: On one side imagine your own "I" which so far has just concentrated on selfish aims. On the other side imagine others—limitless, infinite beings. You yourself are a third person, in the middle, looking at those on either side. As far as the feeling of wanting happiness and not wanting suffering, the two sides are equal, absolutely the same. Also with regard to the right to obtain happiness they are exactly the same. However, no matter how important the selfishly motivated person is, he or she is only one single person; no matter how poor the others are, they are limitless, infinite. The unbiased third person naturally can see that the many are more important than the one. Through this, we can experience, can feel, that the majority—the other limitless beings—are more important than the single person "I."

Thus, the question is: Should everyone be used for my attainment of happiness, or should I be used to gain happiness for others? If I am used for these infinite beings, it is right. If others are used for this single "I," it is absolutely wrong. Even if you can use these others, you will not be happy, whereas if this one single one contributes, serves as much as he or she can, that is a source of great joy. It is in terms of this attitude that real compassion and love for others can be developed.

Compassion that is based on such reasoning and feelings can be extended even to one's enemies. Our ordinary sense of love and compassion is actually very much involved with attachment. For your own wife or husband, your parents, your children, you have a feeling of compassion and love. But because it is in fact related with attachment, it cannot include your enemies. Again it is centered on a selfish motivation—because these are *my* mother, *my* father, *my* children, I love them. In contrast to this is a clear recognition of the importance and rights of others. If compassion is developed from that viewpoint, it will reach even to enemies.

In order to develop such a motivation of compassion, we must have tolerance, patience. In the practice of tolerance, your enemy is the best teacher. Your enemy can teach you tolerance whereas your teacher or parents cannot. Thus from this viewpoint, an enemy is actually helpful—the best of friends, the best of teachers.

In my own experience, the period of greatest gain in knowledge and experience is the most difficult period in one's life. If you go along in an easy way, with everything okay, you feel everything is just fine. Then one day when you encounter problems, you feel depressed and hopeless. Through a difficult period you can learn, you can develop inner strength, determination, and courage to face the problem. Who gives you this chance? Your enemy.

This does not mean that you obey or bow down to your enemy. In fact, sometimes, according to the enemy's attitude, you may have to react strongly—but, deep down, calmness and compassion must not be lost. This is possible. Some people may think, "Now the Dalai Lama is talking nonsense," but I am not. If you practice this, if you test it in your own experience, you can feel it yourself.

The development of love and compassion is basic, and I usually say that this is a main message of religion. When we speak of religion, we need not refer to deeper philosophical issues. Compassion is the real essence of religion. If you try to implement, to practice, compassion, then as a Buddhist, even if you do not place much emphasis on the Buddha, it is all right. For a Christian, if you try to practice this love, there is no need for much emphasis on other philosophical matters. I say this in a friendly way. The important thing is that in your daily life you practice the essential things, and on that level there is hardly any difference between Buddhism, Christianity, or any other religion. All religions emphasize betterment, improving human beings, a sense of brotherhood and sisterhood, love—these things are common. Thus, if you consider the essence of religion, there is not much difference.

I myself feel and also tell other Buddhists that the question of nirvana will come later. There is not much hurry. But if in day to day life you lead a good life, honestly, with love, with compassion, with less selfishness, then automatically it will lead to nirvana. Opposite to this, if we talk about nirvana, talk about philosophy, but do not bother much about day to day practice, then you may reach a strange nirvana but will not reach the correct nirvana because your daily practice is nothing.

We must implement these good teachings in daily life. Whether you believe in God or not does not matter so much; whether you believe in Buddha or not does not matter so much; as a Buddhist, whether you believe in reincarnation or not does not matter so much. You must lead a good life. And a good life does not mean just good food, good clothes, good shelter. These are not sufficient. A good motivation is what is needed: compassion, without dogmatism, without complicated philosophy; just understanding that others are human brothers and sisters and respecting their rights and human dignity. That we humans can help each other is one of our unique human capacities. We must share in other peoples' suffering; even if you cannot help with money, to show concern, to give moral support and express sympathy are themselves valuable. This is what should be the basis of activities; whether one calls it religion or not does not matter.

In the current world atmosphere, some people may think that religion is for those who remain in remote places and is not much needed in the areas of business or politics. My answer to this is "No!" For, as I have just said, in my simple religion, love is the key motivation. Except for certain minor ones, all actions—all larger and deliberate actions—come with motivation. In politics, if you have a good motivation and with that motivation seek to better human society, such a politician is a right and honest politician. Politics itself is not bad. We say, "Dirty politics," but this is not right. Politics is necessary as an instrument to solve human problems, the problems of human society. It itself is not bad; it is necessary. However, if politics are practiced by bad persons, out of cunning and lacking the right motivation, then of course it becomes bad.

This is true not only in politics but in all areas, including religion—if I speak of religion with a bad motivation, that preaching becomes bad. But you cannot say religion is bad; you cannot say, "Dirty religion."

Thus motivation is very important, and thus my simple religion is love, respect for others, honesty: teachings that cover not only religion but also the fields of politics, economy, business, science, law, medicine—everywhere. With proper motivation these can help humanity; without it they go the other way. Without good motivation science and technology, instead of helping, bring more fear and threaten global destruction. Compassionate thought is important for humankind.

At the present moment, if you look more deeply into society, you see that people are not as happy as might first seem. For example, when I first land in a new country, everything is beautiful. When I meet new people, everything is nice, no complaints at all.

But then day by day I listen, I hear people's problems, and it is clear that everywhere there are many problems. Deep down there is unrest. Due to this inner feeling of unrest, people feel isolated, they get depressed, have mental uneasiness, mental suffering. This is the general atmosphere. Real justice and honesty are impossible within cunning feelings. Wanting to benefit others but deep down having a selfish motivation is again impossible. If you talk about peace, love, justice, and so forth, but then when things are actually affecting you, forget all about them and, if necessary, suppress others or even make war, this is a clear sign that something is lacking.

This troubled atmosphere is our current reality. It is very bad, but it is reality. People may feel that the opposite of this, the internal transformation about which I have been speaking, is merely idealistic and not related with our situation here on earth. My feeling, however, is that if this present atmosphere in which everything depends on money and power and there is not much concern about the real value of love continues, if human society loses the value of justice, the value of compassion, the value of honesty, we will in the next generation or farther in the future face greater difficulties and more suffering. Thus, although to bring about inner change is difficult, it is absolutely worthwhile to try. This is my firm belief. What is important is that we try our best. Whether we succeed or not is a different question. Even if we could not achieve what we seek within this life, it is all right; at least we will have made the attempt to form a better human society on the basis of love—true love—and less selfishness.

The people who deal daily with current problems must focus on the immediate problem but at the same time must look at the long-term effect on humankind, on human society. For example, basically, your whole physical body must be healthy and strong, for, with a basis of good health, you will not experience small illnesses or, even if you do, can within a short period easily be cured.

Human society is similar. If we concentrate one hundred percent in the "realistic way" on short-term benefits, on a temporary-benefits-basis, that is like being sick today and taking a pill. If at the same time there is more thought and more discussion about the long-term future of humankind, this is like building a healthy body. It is necessary to combine temporary and long-term handling of problems.

For the last several years I have been looking at the world's problems, including our own problem, the Tibetan situation. I have been thinking about this and meeting with persons from different fields and different countries. Basically all are the same. I come from the East; most of you here are Westerners. If I look at you superficially, we are different, and if I put my emphasis on that level, we grow more distant. If I look on you as my own kind, as human beings like myself, with one nose, two eyes, and so forth, then automatically that distance is gone. We are the same human flesh. I want happiness; you also want happiness. From that mutual recognition we can build respect and real trust for each other. From that can come cooperation and harmony, and from that we can stop many problems.

In this world at the present moment, not just nation to nation, but continent to continent we are heavily dependent upon each other. Hence it is essential that there be true cooperation with good motivation. Then we can solve many problems. Good relations, heart to heart, human to human, are very important and very necessary. Everything depends upon good motivation.

THE LUMINOUS
NATURE OF THE MIND

CLAREMONT COLLEGE, CALIFORNIA

T IS NECESSARY FOR US to familiarize with and get used to good attitudes, but our habituation to bad emotions such as hatred makes a huge obstacle. Thus, we need to identify the various forms of bad afflictive emotions and combat them right on the spot. If you gradually become accustomed to controlling bad attitudes, over a period of years it is possible even for someone who often used to get very angry to become calm.

Some people might feel that you lose your independence if you do not let your mind just wander where it wants to, if you try to control it. This is not so; if your mind is proceeding in a correct way, you already have independence, but if it is proceeding in an incorrect way, it is necessary to exercise control.

Is it possible to get rid of the afflictive emotions completely or is it possible only to suppress them? From the Buddhist point of view, the conventional nature of the mind is clear light, and thus defilements do not reside in the very nature of the mind; defilements are adventitious, temporary, and can be removed. From the ultimate point of view the nature of the mind is its emptiness of inherent existence.

If afflictive emotions, such as hatred, were in the nature of the mind, then from its inception the mind would always have to be hateful, for instance, since that would be its nature. However, that this is not so is obvious; it is only under certain circumstances that we become angry, and when those circumstances are not present, anger is not generated. This indicates that the nature of hatred and the nature of mind are different even if in a deeper sense they both are consciousnesses thus having a nature of luminosity and knowing.

What are the circumstances that serve as a basis for generating hatred? It is generated because we superimpose upon phenomena an unattractiveness or badness that exceeds what is actually there. With this as a basis we get angry at what prevents our desires. Hence, the foundation of a mind of hatred is not valid. However, a mind of love does have a valid foundation. When, over a long period of time, an attitude that has a valid foundation competes with an attitude that does not, the one with the valid foundation will win.

Therefore, if you familiarize steadily over a long period of time with good attitudes that have a valid foundation, bad attitudes that do not will gradually diminish. When training physically in broad-jumping, for instance, the basis of the process is the gross physical body, and thus there is a limit to how much you can jump. However, since the mind is an entity of mere luminosity and knowing, when the basis of training is the mind, it is possible through gradual familiarization to develop salutary attitudes limitlessly.

We ourselves know that the mind can remember many things; putting one thing in mind and then another, it is possible to keep a great amount in memory. Nowadays we cannot maintain an extraordinary amount, but we are using only grosser levels of consciousness; if we utilize more subtle levels, we can retain even more.

Qualities that depend on the mind can be increased limitlessly. As much as you implement and increase the antidotal attitudes that counter afflictive emotions, so much do those unfavorable attitudes decrease, finally being extinguished altogether. Hence, it is said that since we have a mind that has a nature of mere luminosity and knowing, all of us have the fundamental substances necessary for the attainment of Buddhahood.

A basic Buddhist point is that in dependence upon the mind's being essentially an entity of mere luminosity and knowing, it can be shown that the mind can eventually know everything. This, from a philosophical viewpoint, supports the position that good attitudes can be increased limitlessly.

In terms of daily practice it is helpful to identify the conventional nature of the mind and concentrate on it. The reason why it is hard to identify the nature of the mind is that it is as if covered over by our own conceptions. Therefore, first, stop remembering what happened in the past and stop thinking about what might happen in the future; let the mind flow of its own accord without conceptual overlay. Let the mind rest in its natural state, and observe it. In the beginning, when you are not used to this practice, it is quite difficult, but in time the mind appears like clear water. Then, stay with this unfabricated mind without allowing conceptions to be generated.

For this meditation early morning, when your mind has awakened and is clear but your senses are not yet fully operating, is better. It helps not to have eaten too much the night before nor to sleep too much; this makes the mind lighter and sharper the next morning. Gradually the mind will become more and more stable; mindfulness and memory will become clearer.

See if this practice makes your mind more alert throughout the day. As a temporary benefit your thoughts will be tranquil. As your memory improves, gradually you can develop clairvoyance, which is due to an increase of mindfulness. As a long term benefit, because your mind has become more alert and sharp, you can utilize it in whatever field you want.

If you are able to do a little meditation daily, withdrawing this scattered mind on one object inside, it is very helpful. The conceptuality that runs on thinking of good things, bad things, and so forth and so on will get a rest. It provides a little vacation just to sit a bit in non-conceptuality and have a rest.

Four Noble Truths

ALL RELIGIONS HAVE, generally speaking, the same motivation of love and compassion. Though there are often large differences in the philosophical field, the basic goal of improvement is more or less the same. Still, each faith has special methods. Although our cultures are naturally different, our systems are coming closer together because of the world's becoming smaller and smaller with better communication, providing good opportunities for us to learn from each other. This, I feel, is very useful.

For example, Christianity has many practical methods that are useful in the service of humankind, especially in the fields of education and health. Thus, for Buddhists there is much we can learn. At the same time, there are Buddhist teachings on deep meditation and philosophical reasoning from which Christians can learn helpful techniques. In ancient India the Buddhists and Hindus learned many points from each other.

Since these systems basically have the same purpose of benefit for humankind, on the negative side there is nothing wrong with learning from each other, and on the positive side it helps develop respect for each other; it helps promote harmony and unity. For this reason, I will speak a little about Buddhist ideas.

The root of Buddhist doctrine is the four noble truths —true sufferings, sources, cessations, and paths. The four truths are two groups of effect and cause: sufferings and their sources; and cessations of sufferings and the paths for actualizing those cessations. Suffering is like an illness; the external and internal conditions that bring about the illness are the sources of suffering. The state of cure from the illness is the cessation of suffering and of its causes. The medicine that cures the disease is true paths.

The reason for this order with the effects, suffering and cessation, before the causes, sources of suffering and paths, is this: Initially you must identify the illness, true sufferings, the first noble truth. Then, it is not sufficient just to recognize the illness; in order to know which medicine to take it is necessary to know the causes of the illness. Therefore, the second of the four truths is the causes or sources of suffering.

It is not sufficient just to identify the causes of the illness, you need to determine whether it is possible to cure the disease. Knowledge that it can be cured is similar to the third level, that of true cessation of suffering and its causes.

Now, the unwanted suffering has been recognized; its causes have been identified; then, at the point at which it is understood that the illness can be cured, you take the medicines that are the means for removing the illness. Similarly, it is necessary to rely on the paths which will bring about the state of freedom from suffering.

It is considered most important initially to identify suffering. Suffering, in general, is of three types—the suffering of pain, the suffering of change, and pervasive compositional suffering. The suffering of pain is what we usually consider to be physical or mental suffering, for instance, a headache. The wish to be free from this type of suffering occurs not just in humans but also in animals. There are ways of avoiding some forms of this suffering, such as taking medicine, putting on warm clothes, and moving away from the source.

The second level, the suffering of change, is what we super-ficially consider to be pleasure but which, if we look into it, is actually suffering. Take as an example something usually consid-ered to be pleasurable, such as buying a new car. When you first get it, you are very happy, pleased, and satisfied but then as you use it, problems arise. If it were intrinsically pleasurable, no matter how much more you used this cause of satisfaction, your pleasure should increase correspondingly, but such does not happen. As you use it more and more, it begins to cause trouble. Therefore, such things are called sufferings of change; it is through change that their nature of suffering is displayed.

The third level of suffering serves as the basis for the first two, and what illustrates it are our own contaminated mental and phys-ical aggregates. It is called pervasive compositional suffering since it pervades or applies to all types of transmigrating beings and is compositional in that it is the basis of present suffering and induces future suffering. There is no way of getting away from this type of suffering except by ending the continuum of rebirth.

These are the three types of suffering to be identified in the beginning. Thus, not just feelings are identified as suffering but also the external and internal phenomena in dependence upon which such feelings come; the minds and mental factors that accompany them are designated as sufferings as well.

What are the sources of these sufferings? In dependence on what does suffering arise? There are (1) karmic sources and (2) sources that are the afflictive emotions; these are the second of the four noble truths, true sources of suffering. Karma, or action, refers to contaminated physical, verbal, and mental actions. From the point of view of nature or entity, actions are of three types: virtu-ous, non-virtuous, and neutral. Virtuous actions are those that issue forth pleasurable or good effects. Non-virtuous actions are those that issue forth painful or bad effects.

The three main afflictive emotions are obscuration, desire, and hatred. These induce many other varieties of afflictive emotions such as jealousy and enmity. In order to cease the karmas, or actions, that are a source of suffering, it is necessary to cease these afflictive emotions which act as their cause. Therefore, between karma and afflictive emotions the main source of suffering is the latter, afflictive emotions.

When you question whether the afflictive emotions can be removed or not, you are concerned with the third noble truth, true cessations. If afflictive emotions resided in the very nature of the mind, it would be impossible to remove them. If hatred, for example, resided in the nature of the mind, then as long as we are conscious we should be hateful, but this is obviously not the case. The same is true for attachment. Therefore, it is considered that the nature of the mind, of consciousness, is not polluted by defilements. The defilements are susceptible to being removed, suitable to being separated from the basic mind.

It is obvious that the good class of attitudes is contradictory with the bad class of attitudes. For example, love and anger cannot be generated at exactly the same time in the same person. While you are feeling anger with respect to an object, at that very instant you cannot feel love; similarly, while you are feeling love, at that moment you cannot feel anger. This indicates that these two types of consciousnesses are mutually exclusive, contradictory. Thus, naturally, once you become more accustomed to one class of attitudes, the other class becomes weaker and weaker. This is the reason why through practicing and increasing compassion and love—the good side of thought—the other side automatically will diminish.

In this way, it is established that the sources of suffering can gradually be removed. With the utter extinction of the causes of suffering, there is true cessation. This is the final liberation—real, lasting peace, salvation. It is the third of the four noble truths.

In what kind of path should you train to achieve this cessation? Since faults mainly derive from the mind, the antidote must be generated mentally. Indeed, you need to know the final mode of subsistence of all phenomena, but it is most important to know the final status of the mind.

First, you need newly to realize directly and in a totally non-dualistic manner the final nature of the mind exactly as it is; this is called the path of seeing. Then, the next level is to become used to that perception; this is called the path of meditation. Prior to those two levels, it is necessary to achieve a dualistic meditative stabilization which is a union of calm abiding and special insight. Prior to that, generally speaking, in order to have a powerful wisdom consciousness it is necessary first to develop stability of mind, called calm abiding.

These are the levels of the path, the fourth noble truth, required for actualizing the third noble truth, cessations that are states of having ceased the first two noble truths, sufferings and their sources. The four truths are the basic structure of Buddhist thought and practice.

Question: Superficially at least there appears to be a difference between the Buddhist principle of extinguishing desire and the Western importance of having purpose in life, which implies that desire is good.

Answer: There are two types of desire: One type is without reason and is mixed with the afflictive emotions. The second type views what is good as good and seeks to achieve it. This latter type of desire is right, and it is in terms of it that a practitioner engages in practice. Similarly, the pursuit of material progress based on the perception that it can serve humankind and is therefore good is also correct.

KARMA

PLEASURE AND PAIN come from your own former actions (karma). Thus, it is easy to explain karma in one short sentence: If you act well, things will be good, and if you act badly, things will be bad.

Karma means actions. From the viewpoint of how actions are done, there are physical, verbal, and mental actions. From the viewpoint of their effects, actions are either virtuous, non-virtuous, or neutral. In terms of time, there are two types—actions of intention which occur while thinking to do something and the intended actions which are the expressions of those mental motivations in physical or verbal action.

For instance, based on a motive, I am now speaking and thereby accumulating a verbal action or karma. With gestures of my hands, I am also accumulating physical karma. Whether these actions become good or bad is mainly based on my motivation. If I speak from a good motivation out of sincerity, respect, and love for others, my actions are good, virtuous. If I act from a motivation of pride, hatred, criticism, and so forth, then my verbal and physical actions become non-virtuous.

Karmas, therefore, are being made all the time. When one speaks with a good motivation, a friendly atmosphere is created as an immediate result; also, the action makes an imprint on the mind, inducing pleasure in the future. With a bad motivation, a hostile atmosphere is created immediately, and pain is induced for the speaker in the future.

Buddha's teaching is that you are your own master; everything depends on yourself. This means that pleasure and pain arise from virtuous and non-virtuous actions which come not from outside but from within yourself. This theory is useful in daily life, for once you believe in the relationship between actions and their effects, whether there is an external policeman or not, you will always be alert and examine yourself. For example, if there were some money or a precious jewel here and no one around, you could take it easily; however, if you believe in this doctrine, since the whole responsibility for your own future rests on yourself, you will not.

In modern society, despite sophisticated police systems with advanced technology, people still succeed in carrying out deeds of terrorism. Although one side has many sophisticated techniques for keeping track of the other side, that other side is even more sophisticated at making trouble. The only true control is internal—a sense of concern and responsibility for your own future and an altruistic concern for others' well-being.

Practically speaking, the best control of criminality is self-control. Through internal change, crime can be stopped and peace brought to society. Self-examination is most important, and thus the Buddhist theory of self-responsibility is useful as it entails self-examination and self-control in consideration of both one's own and others' interests.

With respect to the effects of actions, many different types are explained. One type is called "effects that are fruitions." For instance, if someone, due to a non-virtuous action, is born in a bad transmigration as an animal, that rebirth is an effect that is a fruition in another life. Another type is called an "effect experientially similar to its cause"; for instance, if after being reborn in a bad transmigration due to an act of murder you were subsequently reborn as a human, you would have a short life—the effect, a short life, being similar in terms of experience to the cause, cutting short someone else's life. Another type is called an "effect functionally similar to its cause"; an example would be naturally to have tendencies toward the same non-virtuous action, such as murder.

Examples for all of these can similarly be applied to virtuous actions. Also, there are actions the effects of which are shared—many beings having similarly done similar types of actions and thereby undergoing effects in common, such as enjoying a certain physical environment together.

The important point is that such presentations of Buddhist theories about actions can make a positive contribution to human society. It is my hope that whether religious or not, we will study each other's systems to gather helpful ideas and techniques for the betterment of humankind.

MEDICINE OF WISDOM
AND COMPASSION

Buddhaṃ sharaṇaṃ gacchāmi.
Dharmaṃ sharaṇaṃ gacchāmi.
Saṅghaṃ sharaṇaṃ gacchāmi.

GO FOR REFUGE to the Buddha, to the Dharma, and to the Sangha." The tune is different from the Tibetan, but the essence is the same, and shows that we are all followers of the same teacher, Buddha. Those of us who chant these prayers believe in the Buddhist teachings, but I cannot say that Buddhism is the best religion for everyone. Various people have various tastes, and so different religions are suitable for different people. Different medicines are prescribed for different diseases, and a medicine appropriate in one situation may be inappropriate in another. Thus, I cannot say of Buddhism simply, "This medicine is best."

The Buddhist teachings are extremely profound as well as varied. Some say of Buddhism that it is not a religion, but rather a science of mind, and some say that Buddhists are atheists. In any case, Buddhism is a rational, deep, and sophisticated approach to human life that does not emphasize something external but rather emphasizes personal responsibility for inner development. Buddha said,

"You are your own master; things depend upon you. I am a teacher, and, like a doctor, I can give you effective medicine, but you have to take it yourself and look after yourself."

Who is Buddha? Buddha is a being who attained complete purification of mind, speech, and body. According to certain scriptures, Buddha's mind, the Dharmakāya, or Truth Body, can be taken as Buddha. Buddha's speech, or inner energy, can be taken as Dharma, the Doctrine. Buddha's physical form can be taken as the Sangha, the Spiritual Community. Thus we return again to the Three Jewels—Buddha, Doctrine, and Spiritual Community.

Is such a Buddha caused or without cause? Caused. Is Buddha permanent? Is Shākyamuni, an individual Buddha, eternal? No. Initially, Shākyamuni Buddha was Siddhārtha, an ordinary being troubled by delusions and engaging in harmful thoughts and wrong actions—someone like ourselves. However, with the help of certain teachings and teachers, he gradually purified himself and in the end became enlightened.

Through this same causal process we too can become fully enlightened. There are many different levels of mind, the most subtle of which is the deep Buddha nature, the seed of Buddhahood. All beings have within them this subtle consciousness, and through the practice of deep meditation and virtuous actions, it gradually can be transformed into pure Buddhahood. Our situation is very hopeful: the seed of liberation is within us.

To be good followers of Buddha we must mainly practice compassion and honesty. Showing kindness to others, we can learn to be less selfish; sharing the sufferings of others, we will develop more concern for the welfare of all beings. This is the basic teaching. To implement this, we practice deep meditation and cultivate wisdom, and as our wisdom develops, our sense of ethics naturally grows stronger.

Buddha always emphasized a balance of wisdom and compassion; a good brain and a good heart should work together. Placing importance just on the intellect and ignoring the heart can create more problems and more suffering in the world. On the other hand, if we emphasize only the heart and ignore the brain, then there is not much difference between humans and animals. These two must be developed in balance, and when they are, the result is material progress accompanied by good spiritual development. Heart and mind working in harmony will yield a truly peaceful and friendly human family.

Question: What does *dharma* mean?

Answer: Dharma is a Sanskrit word that means "hold." From a wide point of view this word can refer to all phenomena because each phenomenon holds its own entity. However, in the context of dharma and the world, dharma refers to any practice through which a person who has it in his or her continuum is held back from a specific fright. This holding back or protection can be from sufferings that are effects or from the causes of those sufferings, the afflictive emotions. We are seeking to control the mind, and those practices through which the mind is controlled are dharma. They hold one back temporarily from fright, and they also hold one back in the long run from frightful or bad situations that would be produced by entering into afflictive emotions.

ALTRUISM AND THE SIX PERFECTIONS

THE MAIN THEME of Buddhism is altruism based on compassion and love. The feeling of compassion is important whether you are a believer or a non-believer, for everyone shares or feels the value of love. When we human beings are small children, we very much depend on the kindness of our parents; without their kindness it would be difficult to survive. Again, when we become old, we very much need the kindness of others—we are dependent on it. Between those two—childhood and old age—we are quite independent, feeling that since we have no need to depend on others, we ourselves do not need to practice kindness. This is wrong.

Those engaged in the practice of compassion feel much happier internally—more calm, more peaceful—and other people reciprocate that feeling. Through anger real peace, friendship, and trust are impossible, but through love we can develop understanding, unity, friendship, and harmony. Thus, kindness and compassion are the most important things, precious and valuable.

We human beings have a sophisticated brain as a result of which we have developed much material progress. However, if we balance external development with internal development, we can utilize material things in the right way. At the same time as we enjoy material progress, we will not lose the value of humanity.

Because compassion and altruism are so important, I will explain a little from the Buddhist teaching on how to practice them. The type of good attitude about which I am speaking is a feeling, when faced with choosing your own or others' welfare, to choose others' welfare rather than your own. Cherishing others' interests and neglecting your own cannot be developed immediately; training is needed. In Buddhism there are two main techniques for developing such an altruistic attitude, one called the equalizing and switching of self and other and another called the sevenfold quintessential instructions of cause and effect. For the first the theory of rebirth is not necessary, whereas for the latter it is. As I have explained the first elsewhere (see pp. 17ff.), I will talk about the sevenfold quintessential instructions of cause and effect today.

In order to have strong consideration for others' happiness and welfare, it is necessary to have a special altruistic attitude in which you take upon yourself the burden of helping others. In order to generate such an unusual attitude, it is necessary to have great compassion, caring about the suffering of others and wanting to do something about it. In order to have such a strong force of compassion, first you must have a strong sense of love which, upon observing suffering sentient beings, wishes that they have happiness—finding a pleasantness in everyone and wishing happiness for everyone just as a mother does for her sole sweet child. Again, in order to have a sense of closeness and dearness for others, you must first train in acknowledging their kindness through using as a model a person in this lifetime who was very kind to yourself and then extending this sense of gratitude to all beings. Since, in general, in this life your mother was the closest and offered the most help, the process of meditation begins with recognizing all other sentient beings as like your mother.

This system of meditation, therefore, has seven steps:

1 recognizing all sentient beings as mothers
2 becoming mindful of their kindness
3 developing an intention to repay their kindness
4 love
5 compassion
6 the unusual attitude
7 the altruistic intention to become enlightened.

To do this meditation, it is necessary to know about the process of rebirth. The final reason showing that there is rebirth is that your consciousness, being an entity of mere luminosity and knowing, must be produced from a former moment of consciousness—from a former entity of luminosity and knowing. It is not possible for consciousness to be produced from matter as its substantial cause. Once consciousness is produced from a former moment of consciousness, a beginning to the continuum of consciousness cannot be posited. In this way, the general and most subtle type of consciousness has no beginning and no end; from this, rebirth is established.

Since rebirths are perforce beginningless, everyone has had a relationship with yourself like that of your own mother of this lifetime. In order to train in such recognition, it is necessary first to have a mind of equanimity. You begin by noting that within our minds we have three main categories for others—friends, enemies, and neutral beings. We have three different attitudes towards them: desire, hatred, and a neglecting indifference. When these three attitudes are generated, it is impossible to generate an altruistic attitude; therefore, it is important to neutralize desire, hatred, and indifference.

To do this, it helps to reflect on rebirth. Since our births are beginningless, there is no limit to their number; thus, it is not definite that those who are now our friends were always friends in the past and that those who are now our enemies were always enemies in the past. Even in terms of this one lifetime, there are persons who early in your life were enemies but later on turned into friends and others who were friends early in the life but later on became enemies. Hence, there is no sense in one-pointedly considering a certain person to be just a friend and another person to be just an enemy.

When you contemplate in this manner, the one-pointed apprehension of some persons as friends and others as enemies and the consequent generation of desire and hatred will become weaker in strength. Imagine in front of yourself three people—a friend, an enemy, and a neutral person—and, while observing them, consider that there is no certainty that any one of them will at all times either help or harm. It is important to do this meditation with regard to specific persons and not just all sentient beings in general, the latter being too vague for a change of attitude to apply to specific people. Gradually, a sense of equanimity will develop toward these three, after which you can extend this feeling slowly toward other beings.

When you have undergone this change, the next step is to consider that since everyone's births have been beginningless and thus limitless in number, every single person has been your best of friends, parent or whatever, over the course of lifetimes. Taking this realization as a basis, you can slowly develop an attitude considering all sentient beings to be friends.

Then, consider the kindness that they individually afforded to you when they were your parents. When they were your mother or father, usually the best of all friends, they protected you with kindness just as your parents in this lifetime did when you were small. Since there is no difference in the fact that people have been kind to you whether they expressed that kindness recently or a while ago, all beings have equally shown kindness to you either in this lifetime or in other lifetimes; they are all equally kind.

Also, even when others were not your parents, they were very kind to you. This is because most of the good qualities that we have are produced in dependence upon other persons. As I will be explaining later, the practice of the six perfections depends almost entirely on other sentient beings. Similarly, in the initial practice of ethics, in the abandonment of the ten non-virtues— killing, stealing, sexual misconduct, lying, divisive talk, harsh speech, senseless chatter, covetousness, harmful intent, and wrong views—these are mostly done in relation to other sentient beings. In addition, even in our present lifetime, all these many facilities that we enjoy—nice buildings, roads, and so forth—are produced by other people. Also, in order to become enlightened you have to engage in the important practice of patience, and in order to practice patience you need an enemy; thus enemies are valuable.

If you consider the matter in depth and in detail, even great enemies who for a period of time single-pointedly harmed you extended great kindness to you. The reason for this is that from an enemy you can learn real tolerance and patience whereas from a religious teacher or your parents the strength of your tolerance cannot be tested. Only when faced with the activity of enemies can you learn real inner strength. From this viewpoint, even enemies are teachers of inner strength, courage, and determination. Due to having an enemy, you also may come closer to reality, peeling off pretensions.

When altruism is practiced, enemies are not to be neglected but should be cherished even more. So, instead of getting angry at your enemies you should think to repay their kindness, for one should repay any kindness that has been extended to oneself. If you did not repay it, it would be vulgar.

After becoming mindful of others' kindness, a feeling to repay that kindness comes. How is it to be repaid? The next step is to generate a sense of love, wishing for the happiness of all sentient beings, wishing that beings bereft of happiness have happiness and all of its causes. As much as you view sentient beings with love, finding a sense of pleasantness in everyone and cherishing them, so much do you generate the next step, compassion, which is a wish that they be free from suffering and all of its causes.

The generation of love and compassion involves a change of attitude on your own part, but the beings who are the objects of these feelings are still left suffering. So, having generated love and compassion, the next step is to extend these altruistic attitudes beyond just the thought, "How nice it would be if they were free from suffering and its causes and came to possess happiness and its causes," and develop the stronger thought, "I will cause them to be free from suffering and its causes and to be endowed with happiness and its causes." Here, you develop the strong determination not just to generate such good attitudes in mind but actually to free those beings from suffering and establish them in happiness through your own effort.

This high intention will endow you with great courage to take on the great burden of all sentient beings' welfare. When you have this strength of mind, as great as the hardships are, so great will become your sense of determination and courage. Hardship will assist your determination.

Not only for practitioners of religion but also for other people, courage is important. The saying that where there is a will there is a way is indeed true. If when we get into a difficult situation our will or courage lessens and we fall into the laziness of feeling inferior, thinking that we could not possibly accomplish such a difficult task, this diminishment of will cannot protect us from any suffering. It is important to generate courage corresponding to the size of the difficulties.

The helping of others refers not just to giving food, shelter, and so forth but also to relieving the basic causes of suffering and providing the basic causes of happiness. For instance, in society usually we do not just give food and clothing to people but try to educate them so that they can develop to the point where they can take care of their own lives. Similarly, in the Bodhisattva practices one does not just give persons temporary material things to relieve them of poverty but also teaches them, so that they themselves will know what to adopt in practice and what to discard from within their behavior.

In order to teach these things to others, first it is necessary to know persons' dispositions and interests as well as to know the beneficial doctrines exactly as they are without omission or error. To help others, you must have many capacities. Therefore, as a branch of the process of helping others, it is necessary to achieve the enlightenment in which the obstructions preventing realization of all objects of knowledge are utterly removed.

For a Bodhisattva who is seeking to help others, from among the obstructions to liberation and obstructions to omniscience, the obstructions to omniscience are worse; they are what a Bodhisattva wants to get rid of most of all. In fact, there are even cases of Bodhisattvas using afflictive emotions, which are obstructions to liberation, to aid others. Nevertheless, since the obstructions to omniscience are predispositions established by the conception of inherent existence (the chief of the obstructions to liberation), it is necessary first to remove that conception of inherent existence. Hence, for a Bodhisattva to accomplish others' welfare in a complete way, it is necessary to remove both obstructions, those to liberation and those to omniscience.

The complete removal of the afflictive obstructions is called liberation; this is the state of a Foe Destroyer (*arhan, dgra bcom pa*). The removal, in addition, of the obstructions to omniscience is called Buddhahood, a state of omniscience; this is sought in order to be of full use to others. A mind which, for the sake of sentient beings, seeks to achieve such highest enlightenment is called a mind of enlightenment—an altruistic intention to become enlightened. Generation of this attitude is the last of the seven cause and effect quintessential instructions.[2]

Within Buddhism this is the best of all altruistic attitudes. When this altruism is transformed into action, you engage in practicing the six perfections: giving, ethics, patience, effort, concentration, and wisdom. There are three types of giving—the giving of resources, of one's own body, and of roots of virtue. It is the most difficult to give away your own roots of virtue, and it is also the most important. When you have a strong sense of giving and dedicating to others your roots of virtue, you no longer seek for any reward for yourself. Even though mere giving can be done by those seeking their own benefit, a Bodhisattva's giving is not involved in selfishness at all.

There are many types of ethics, but with regard to the Bodhisattva ethics the main practice is to refrain from or to restrain selfishness. In Sanskrit, the word "ethics" is *shīla*, which is etymologized as meaning "attainment of coolness." When persons possess ethics, their minds have a peacefulness or coolness free from the heat of regretting what they have done.

With respect to patience, there is the patience of not worrying about harm from an enemy as well as the patience that is voluntary assumption of suffering and the patience of bringing about the welfare of sentient beings. The patience that is the voluntary assumption of suffering is very important. It is a case of not withering in the face of suffering and serves as a basis for increasing effort in order to oppose the roots of suffering.

Effort is crucial in the beginning for generating a strong will. We all have the Buddha nature and thus already have within us the substances through which, when we meet with the proper conditions, we can turn into a fully enlightened being having all beneficial attributes and devoid of all faults. The very root of failure in our lives is to think, "Oh, how useless and powerless I am!" It is important to have a strong force of mind thinking, "I can do it," this not being mixed with pride or any other afflictive emotion.

Moderate effort over a long period of time is important, no matter what you are trying to do. One brings failure on oneself by working extremely hard at the beginning, attempting to do too much, and then giving it all up after a short time. A constant stream of moderate effort is needed. Similarly, when meditating, you need to be skillful by having frequent, short sessions; it is more important that the session be of good quality than that it be long.

When you have such effort, you have the necessary "substances" for developing concentration. Concentration is a matter of channeling this mind which is presently distracted in a great many directions. A scattered mind does not have much power. When channeled, no matter what the object of observation is, the mind is very powerful.

There is no external way to channel the mind, as by a surgical operation; it must be done by withdrawing it inside. Withdrawal of the mind also occurs in deep sleep in which the factor of alertness has become unclear; therefore, here the withdrawal of the mind is to be accompanied by strong clarity of alertness. In brief, the mind must have stability staying firmly on its object, great clarity of the object, and alert, clear, sharp tautness.

With respect to the last perfection, wisdom, there are in general many types of wisdom; the three main ones are conventional wisdom realizing the five fields of knowledge, ultimate wisdom realizing the mode of subsistence of phenomena, and wisdom knowing how to help sentient beings. The main one being explained here is the second, the wisdom realizing selflessness.

With regard to selflessness, it is necessary to know what "self" is—to identify the self that does not exist. Then one can understand its opposite, selflessness. Selflessness is not a case of something that existed in the past becoming non-existent; rather, this sort of "self" is something that never did exist. What is needed is to identify as non-existent something that always was non-existent, for due to not having made such identification, we are drawn into the afflictive emotions of desire and hatred as well as all the problems these bring.

What is this self that does not exist? In this context, "self" refers not to the person or "I" as it usually does but to independence, something that exists under its own power. You should examine all types of phenomena to determine if they exist under their own power, to see whether they have their own independent mode of subsistence or not. If phenomena do exist under their own power, then when you investigate to find the object designated, it should become clearer and clearer.

For instance, consider your own person (the usual type of "self") or "I." The "I" appears from within the context of mind and body; however, if you investigate these places from which it appears, you cannot find it. Similarly, with regard to this which we point out as a table, if you are not satisfied with its mere appearance but investigate its nature, searching among its various parts and separating out all of its qualities and so forth, there is no table left to be found as the substrate of those parts and qualities.

The fact that things are not findable under analysis when you search to find the object designated indicates that phenomena do not exist under their own power. Objects are not established objectively in and of themselves but do indeed exist; even if under analysis I search to find the table and cannot find it, if I hit it with my fist, it will hurt my knuckles. Thus, its existence is indicated by my own experience. However, that it cannot be found under analysis indicates that it does not exist in its own objective right, and thus since it exists, it is said to exist through the power of a subjective conventional consciousness.

That objects exist in dependence upon a subjective designating consciousness is the same as saying that they are only nominally existent. Therefore, with respect to your "I" or person, when you search to find it among its bases of designation, mind and body, it cannot be found, and thus there is just the mere "I" that exists through the force of conceptuality.

How things appear and how they actually exist differ greatly. A person engaging in practice of the perfection of wisdom does this kind of analysis and then examines how things appear in ordinary experience, alternating analysis and comparison with the usual mode of appearance in order to notice the discrepancy between the actual mode of subsistence of phenomena and their appearance.

In this way the inherent existence which is the object of negation will become clearer and clearer. As much as the object of negation becomes clearer, so much deeper will your understanding of emptiness become. Finally, you will ascertain a mere vacuity that is a negative of inherent existence.

Since emptiness, from between positive and negative phenomena, is a negative phenomenon and, from between affirming negatives and non-affirming negatives, is a non-affirming negative, when it appears to the mind, nothing will appear except an absence of such inherent existence—a mere elimination of the object of negation. Thus, for the mind of a person realizing emptiness there is no sense of, "I am ascertaining emptiness," and there is no thought, "This is emptiness." If you had such a sense, emptiness would become distant. Nevertheless, the emptiness of inherent existence is ascertained and realized.

After such realization, even though whatever phenomena appear

appear to exist in their own right, you understand that they do not exist that way. You have a sense that they are like a magician's illusions in that there is a combination of their appearing one way but actually existing another way. Though they appear to exist inherently, you understand that they are empty of inherent existence.

When phenomena are seen this way, the conceptions that superimpose a sense of goodness or badness on phenomena beyond what is actually there and serve as a basis for generating desire and hatred lessen; this is because they are based on the misconception that phenomena are established in their own right. On the other hand, those consciousnesses that have a valid foundation increase in strength. The reason for this is that the meaning of emptiness is the meaning of dependent-arising. Since phenomena are dependent-arisings, they are capable of increase and decrease in dependence upon conditions.

In this way, cause and effect are feasible, positable, and once cause and effect are validly positable, it can be posited that bad effects such as suffering can be avoided by abandoning bad causes and that good effects such as happiness can be achieved by training in good causes. If, on the other hand, phenomena did exist in their own right, they would not depend on others, and if they did not depend on others, cause and effect would be impossible. Thus, once dependence is feasible, causes and effect can be posited, and if dependence were not feasible, causes and effects could not exist.

The final reason proving that things are empty of inherent existence is just this dependence on causes and conditions. When people do not understand this doctrine well, they mistakenly think that because phenomena are empty, there is no good and bad, no cause and effect. This is complete misunderstanding.

It is so important to be able to posit and have conviction in cause and effect that it is said that between giving up belief in the cause and effect of actions and giving up belief in emptiness, it is better to give up the doctrine of emptiness. Also, due to the importance of having belief in cause and effect, various explanations of emptiness are given in the Middle Way and Mind-Only Schools. In some systems of tenets it is even accepted that phenomena inherently exist because without analytically findable existence many persons cannot posit cause and effect for the time being.

Knowledge of the final mode of subsistence of phenomena must be within the context of not losing the cause and effect of actions conventionally; if in an attempt to understand the final mode of subsistence one lost the presentation of conventionally existent cause and effect, the purpose would be defeated. Just as children must go to primary, secondary, and high school before going to college or university—proceeding to the higher levels based on the lower—so, it is in dependence on having gained ascertainment with respect to the cause and effect of actions that later the profound view of the emptiness of inherent existence is ascertained without losing the earlier conviction in cause and effect and its consequent practices.

If someone thought that because phenomena are empty there could not be any good or bad, even if that person repeated the word "emptiness" a thousand times, he or she would be moving farther and farther away from the meaning of emptiness. Hence, a person who has great interest in emptiness should pay great heed to the cause and effect of actions.

That, in brief, is the practice of the perfection of wisdom. These six perfections are the heart of a Bodhisattva's implementation of altruism.

RELIGIOUS HARMONY

. . .

THAT WE HAVE HERE a common gathering of various believers is a positive sign. Among spiritual faiths, there are many different philosophies, some just opposite to each other on certain points. Buddhists do not accept a creator; Christians base their philosophy on that theory. There are great differences, but I deeply respect your faith, not just for political reasons or to be polite, but sincerely. For many centuries your tradition has given great service to humankind.

We Tibetans have benefited greatly from the help offered by Christian relief organizations, such as the World Council of Churches, as well as the many others that have helped Tibetan refugees when we were passing through our most difficult period. Our Christian friends all over the world showed us great sympathy along with substantial material assistance, and I would like to express my deepest thanks to them all.

All of the different religious communities accept that there is another force beyond the reach of our ordinary senses. When we pray together, I feel something, I do not know what the exact word is—whether you would call it blessings, or grace—but in any case there is a certain feeling that we can experience. If we utilize it properly, that feeling is helpful for inner strength. For a real sense of brotherhood and sisterhood that feeling—that atmosphere and experience—is very useful and helpful. Therefore I particularly appreciate this ecumenical gathering.

All of the different religious faiths, despite their philosophical differences, have a similar objective. Every religion emphasizes human improvement, love, respect for others, sharing other peoples' suffering. On these lines every religion has more or less the same viewpoint and the same goal.

Those faiths that emphasize Almighty God and faith in and love of God have as their purpose the fulfillment of God's intentions. Seeing us all as creations of and followers of one God, they teach that we should cherish and help each other. The very purpose of faithful belief in God is to accomplish His wishes, the essence of which is to cherish, respect, love, and give service to our fellow humans.

Since an essential purpose of other religions is similarly to promote such beneficial feelings and actions, I strongly feel that from this viewpoint a central purpose of all the different philosophical explanations is the same. Through the various religious systems, followers are assuming a salutary attitude toward their fellow humans—our brothers and sisters—and implementing this good motivation in the service of human society. This has been demonstrated by a great many believers in Christianity throughout history; many have sacrificed their lives for the benefit of humankind. This is true implementation of compassion.

When we Tibetans were passing through a difficult period, Christian communities from all over the world took it upon themselves to share our suffering and rushed to our help. Without regard for racial, cultural, religious, or philosophical differences, they regarded us as fellow humans and came to help. This gave us real inspiration and recognition of the value of love.

Love and kindness are the very basis of society. If we lose these feelings, society will face tremendous difficulties; the survival of humanity will be endangered. Together with material development, we need spiritual development so that inner peace and social harmony can be experienced. Without inner peace, without inner calm, it is difficult to have lasting peace. In this field of inner development religion can make important contributions.

Although in every religion there is an emphasis on compassion and love, from the viewpoint of philosophy, of course there are differences, and that is all right. Philosophical teachings are not the end, not the aim, not what you serve. The aim is to help and benefit others, and philosophical teachings to support those ideas are valuable. If we go into the differences in philosophy and argue with and criticize each other, it is useless. There will be endless argument; the result will mainly be that we irritate each other— accomplishing nothing. Better to look at the purpose of the philosophies and to see what is shared—an emphasis on love, compassion, and respect for a higher force.

No religion basically believes that material progress alone is sufficient for humankind. All religions believe in forces beyond material progress. All agree that it is important and worthwhile to make strong effort to serve human society.

To do this, it is important that we understand each other. In the past, due to narrow-mindedness and other factors, there has sometimes been discord between religious groups. This should not happen again. If we look deeply into the value of a religion in the context of the worldwide situation, we can easily transcend these unfortunate happenings. For there are many areas of common ground on which we can have harmony. Let us just be side by side —helping, respecting, and understanding each other—in common effort to serve humankind. The aim of human society must be the compassionate betterment of human beings.

Politicians and world leaders are trying their best to achieve arms control and so forth, and this is useful. At the same time, we who have certain beliefs have a duty and responsibility to control our own bad thoughts. This is the real disarmament, our own arms control. With inner peace and full control of bad thoughts, external control is not particularly significant. Without inner control, no matter what steps are taken, external efforts will not make much difference. Therefore, under the present circumstances, we in the religious community have a special responsibility to all humanity—a universal responsibility.

The world situation is such that continent to continent all are heavily dependent on each other, and under such circumstances genuine cooperation is essential. This depends on good motivation. That is our universal responsibility.

Question: As a religious leader, are you interested in actively encouraging others to join your faith? Or do you take the position of being available if someone should seek knowledge of your faith?

Answer: This is an important question. I am interested not in converting other people to Buddhism but in how we Buddhists can contribute to human society, according to our own ideas. I believe that other religious faiths also think in a similar way, seeking to contribute to the common aim.

Because the different religions have at times argued with each other rather than concentrating on how to contribute to a common aim, for the last twenty years in India I have taken every occasion to meet with Christian monks—Catholic and Protestant—as well as Muslims and Jews and, of course, in India, many Hindus. We meet, pray together, meditate together, and discuss their philosophical ideas, their way of approach, their techniques. I take great interest in Christian practices, what we can learn and copy from their system. Similarly, in Buddhist theory there may be points such as meditative techniques which can be practiced in the Christian church.

Just as Buddha showed an example of contentment, tolerance, and serving others without selfish motivation, so did Jesus Christ. Almost all of the great teachers lived a saintly life—not luxuriously like kings or emperors but as simple human beings. Their inner strength was tremendous, limitless, but the external appearance was of contentment with a simple way of life.

Question: Can there be a synthesis of Buddhism, Judaism, Christianity, Hinduism, and all religions, gathering the best in all, and forming a world religion?

Answer: Forming a new world religion is difficult and not particularly desirable. However, in that love is essential to all religions, one could speak of the universal religion of love. As for the techniques and methods for developing love as well as for achieving salvation or permanent liberation, there are many differences between religions. Thus, I do not think we could make one philosophy or one religion.

Furthermore, I think that differences in faith are useful. There is a richness in the fact that there are so many different presentations of the way. Given that there are so many different types of people with various predispositions and inclinations, this is helpful.

At the same time, the motivation of all religious practice is similar—love, sincerity, honesty. The way of life of practically all religious persons is contentment. The teachings of tolerance, love, and compassion are the same. A basic goal is the benefit of humankind—each type of system seeking in its own unique ways to improve human beings. If we put too much emphasis on our own philosophy, religion, or theory, are too attached to it, and try to impose it on other people, it makes trouble. Basically all the great teachers, such as Gautama Buddha, Jesus Christ, or Mohammed, founded their new teachings with a motivation of helping their fellow humans. They did not mean to gain anything for themselves nor to create more trouble or unrest in the world.

Most important is that we respect each other and learn from each other those things that will enrich our own practice. Even if all the systems are separate, since they each have the same goal, the study of each other is helpful.

Question: Sometimes when we hear Eastern religions compared with Western culture, the West is made to seem materialistic and less enlightened than the East. Do you see such a difference?

Answer: There are two kinds of food—food for mental hunger and food for physical hunger. Thus a combination of these two —material progress and spiritual development—is the most practical thing. I think that many Americans, particularly young Americans, realize that material progress alone is not the full answer for human life. Right now all of the Eastern nations are trying to copy Western technology. We Easterners such as Tibetans, like myself, look to Western technology feeling that once we develop material progress, our people can reach some sort of permanent happiness. But when I come to Europe or North America, I see that underneath the beautiful surface there is still unhappiness, mental unrest, and restlessness. This shows that material progress alone is not the full answer for human beings.

TREASURES OF
TIBETAN BUDDHISM

ASIA SOCIETY, NEW YORK CITY

I THINK THAT, briefly speaking, there is within Tibetan Buddhism the complete practice of all of Buddhism. As all of you know, within Buddhism there are the designations of the Vehicle of Hearers and the Vehicle of Bodhisattvas. Within the latter, there is a division into the Vehicle of the Perfections and the Vehicle of Secret Mantra, or Tantra. In Ceylon, Burma, and Thailand, the type of Buddhism that is practiced is Theravāda. It is one of the four main divisions of the Great Exposition School (*vaibhāṣika, bye brag smra ba*) school of tenets—Mahāsaṃghika, Sarvāstivāda, Saṃmitīya, and Sthaviravāda or Theravāda.

Among Tibetans, the transmission of the monks' vows stems from one of these divisions of the Great Exposition School, the Sarvāstivāda. Due to the fact that there are these different sub-schools, the Theravādins follow a system of discipline in which there are two hundred twenty-seven vows, whereas we who follow the Sarvāstivāda discipline have two hundred fifty-three.

Except for these slight differences, both are the same in being Hearer Vehicle systems. Therefore, we Tibetans are practicing the Hearer Vehicle form of discipline, this covering the full range of activities related with discipline, from the time of taking the vows, to the precepts that are kept, to the rites that are used in the maintenance of these vows.

Similarly, we also practice the modes of generating meditative stabilization as they are set forth in Vasubandhu's *Treasury of Manifest Knowledge* (*abhidharmakośa, chos mngon pa'i mdzod*), a Hearer Vehicle compendium, as well as the thirty-seven harmonies with enlightenment [a central part of Hearer Vehicle path structure]. Therefore, in Tibetan Buddhism we engage in practices that are completely in accord with Theravāda modes of practice.

The doctrines of the Great Vehicle spread widely to countries such as China, Japan, Korea, and some parts of Indochina. These doctrines, embodying the Bodhisattva Vehicle, are based on specific sūtras such as the *Heart Sūtra* or *Lotus Sūtra*. In the Great Vehicle scriptural collections, the basis or root is the generation of the altruistic aspiration to Buddhahood and its attendant practices, these being the six perfections. In terms of the view of emptiness, there are two different schools of tenets within the Great Vehicle—the Mind-Only School (*cittamātra, sems tsam pa*) and the Middle Way School (*mādhyamika, dbu ma pa*). These Great Vehicle modes of practice of compassion and wisdom are also present in complete form within Tibetan Buddhism.

With respect to the Mantra or Tantra Vehicle, it is clear that its doctrines spread to China and Japan. However, within the division of the Tantra Vehicle into the four sets of tantras—Action, Performance, Yoga, and Highest Yoga Tantra, only the first three—Action, Performance, and Yoga—spread there. It appears that Highest Yoga Tantra did not reach China and Japan, although there might have been cases of its secret practice. However, with respect to the tantras brought into Tibet, in addition to the three lower tantric systems, Action, Performance, and Yoga, there are many tantras of the Highest Yoga class.

Thus, the practice of Buddhism in Tibet includes a complete

form of practice of all systems within Buddhism—Hearer Vehicle, Sūtra Great Vehicle, and Mantra Great Vehicle. The mode of
practicing a union of sūtra and tantra in complete form spread
from Tibet to the Mongol areas—including Inner Mongolia,
Outer Mongolia, the Kalmyk peoples, and so forth. It also spread
to the Himalayan regions including Nepal, Sikkim, and Bhutan.

Thus, the Tibetan form of Buddhism is complete. I say this not
to show off but in hope that you will gradually look into the matter and discover it yourself.

There are four schools or orders of Tibetan Buddhism: Nyingma, Kagyu, Sakya, and Geluk. Each of these, in turn, has many
divisions. Nyingma, for instance, presents nine vehicles—three
sūtra systems and six tantra systems. Also, within Nyingma there
are systems derived from discovered texts. Despite the fact that one
can make such differences among even the four schools of Tibetan
Buddhism, each is a system of complete practice of a unification
of sūtra and tantra. This is because in terms of their view of the
way things are in reality, each of these systems holds the view of
the Middle Way Consequence School (*prāsaṅgika-mādhyamika,
dbu ma thal 'gyur pa*), and in terms of motivation and altruistic
deeds, all follow the system of generating the altruistic intention
to become enlightened and practicing the six perfections.

What is the mode of practice by which one person can simultaneously engage in the practice of the union of sūtra and tantra?
It is said that externally, one should abide within the behavior that
accords with the Hearer Vehicle discipline. For instance, even
Tibetan yogis who practice tantra as laypersons assume the vows
of a Hearer Vehicle layperson and externally maintain a life-style
that accords with that discipline. Then, internally, one needs to
train in and develop the mind of the altruistic intention to gain
enlightenment which has as its roots love and compassion. Then
secretly, through the practice of deity yoga, one engages in con-

centration on the channels, essential drops, and winds, in order to enhance progress on the path.

In Tibet, we see all these aspects of practice as compatible; we do not view sūtra and tantra as contradictory, like hot and cold; we do not consider that the practice of the view of emptiness and the practice of altruistic deeds are contradictory at all. As a result of this, we are able to combine all of the systems into a single unified practice.

To summarize, the altruistic intention to become enlightened is the root, or basis, of the vast series of compassionate practices. The doctrine of emptiness is the root of the practices of the profound view. In order to develop the mind that realizes the suchness of phenomena higher and higher, it is necessary to engage in meditation. In order to achieve meditative stabilization and bring great force to these practices, there is the special practice of deity yoga, for in dependence on deity yoga, it is possible to achieve easily a meditative stabilization that is a union of calm abiding and special insight. As the basis for such practice, it is necessary to keep good ethics. Thus, the complete system of practice in Tibet is explained as externally maintaining a Hearer Vehicle system of ethics, internally maintaining the Sūtra Great Vehicle generation of altruism, love, compassion, and secretly maintaining the practice of the Mantra Vehicle.

Having explained a little about the general outline of the type of practice, I will now say a bit about the practice itself. The root of all the Buddhist and non-Buddhist systems which appeared in India is that people were seeking happiness, and within the division of the phenomena of the world into objects that are used and the user of those objects, the Indians put particular emphasis on the self which uses objects. Most of the non-Buddhist systems, based on the fact that it often appears to our minds that the self is the controller of mind and body or that the self is undergoing pleasure and pain which in some sense appear to be separate from it, came to the conclusion that there is a separate self, a different entity from mind and body, which is the factor that goes from lifetime to lifetime and takes rebirth.

However, Buddhists do not assert that there is a self that is completely separate, or a different entity, from mind and body. Thus, they do not assert a permanent, single, independent self. This is because the four seals that testify to a doctrine as being Buddhist are that (1) all products are impermanent, (2) all contaminated things are miserable, (3) all phenomena are empty of self, and (4) nirvana is peace.

Since within the Buddhist systems there is no self completely separate from mind and body, there come to be different assertions within those systems on how the self is found within the mental and physical aggregates. In the systems of the Middle Way Autonomy School (*svātantrika-mādhyamika, dbu ma rang rgyud pa*), Mind-Only School, Sūtra School (*sautrāntika, mdo sde pa*), and Great Exposition School, a factor from within the mental and physical aggregates is posited as that which is the self. However, in the highest system of tenets, the Middle Way Consequence School, nothing from within the mental and physical aggregates is posited as the illustration of, or that which is, the self.

In this highest of systems, as in the others, there is an assertion of selflessness, but this does not mean that there is no self at all. In the Middle Way Consequence School it means that when we search to find the kind of self that appears to our minds so concretely, we cannot find it. Such a self is analytically unfindable. Analytical findability is called "inherent existence"; thus, when the Middle Way Consequence School speaks of selflessness, they are referring to this lack of inherent existence. However, they do assert that there is a self, or "I," or person that is designated in dependence upon mind and body.

All Buddhist systems assert *pratītya-samutpāda,* dependent-arising. One meaning of the doctrine of dependent-arising is that all impermanent things—products, or things that are made—arise in dependence upon an aggregation of causes and conditions; therefore, they arise dependently. The second meaning of dependent-arising, however, is that phenomena are designated, or come into being, in dependence upon the collection of their own parts. The breaking down of phenomena by scientists into extremely small particles serves to support this doctrine that phenomena are designated in dependence upon a collection of parts, these parts being their minute particles. A third meaning of dependent-arising is that phenomena only nominally exist. This means that phenomena do not exist in and of themselves objectively but depend upon subjective designation for their existence. When it is said that phenomena exist or are designated in dependence upon a conceptual consciousness—which designates them as this or that—we are not saying that there are no objects external to the consciousnesses perceiving them as is asserted in the Mind-Only system. There it is said that phenomena are only mental appearances, but again not that forms and so forth do not exist, rather that they do not exist as external objects—objects external in entity to the mind. In this way the meaning of dependent-arising becomes deeper and deeper in these three descriptions.

Because the self, which is the user or enjoyer of objects, exists in dependence upon other factors, that self is not independent, but dependent. Since it is impossible for the self to be independent, it is completely devoid of independence. This lack of independence of the self that undergoes pleasure and pain and so forth is its reality, its emptiness of inherent existence. This is what emptiness is getting at. Through understanding and feeling the meaning of this doctrine you can begin to gain control over your emotions in daily life.

Unfavorable emotions arise from superimposing upon objects a goodness or badness beyond that which they actually have. We are putting on something extra, and in reaction to this, unfavorable emotions arise. For instance, when we generate desire or hatred, at that time we are seeing something very attractive or very unattractive strongly in front of us, objectively. But then if we look at it later, it just makes us laugh; the same feeling is not there. Therefore, the objects of desire and hatred involve a superimposition beyond what actually exists; something else has become mixed in. This is how understanding the actual mode of being of objects without such superimpositions helps us to control our minds.

This is the factor of wisdom, but there is also a factor of method. For what purpose are we striving to generate wisdom? If it is for your own selfish purposes, then it cannot become very powerful. Therefore, wisdom must be accompanied by a motivation of love, of compassion, of mercy for others, such that it is put to the use of others. In this way, there comes to be a union of method and wisdom. Love, when it is not mixed with false conceptuality, is reasonable, logical, sensible.

Loving-kindness and compassion, without emotional feelings and with the realization of ultimate reality, can reach even your enemy. This love is even stronger for your enemies. The other kind of love, without realization of reality, is very close to attachment; it cannot reach enemies—only friends, your wife, husband, children, parents, and so forth. Such love and kindness are biased. Realization of the ultimate nature assists in making love or kindness become principled and pure.

Such a union of wisdom and method is to be brought into daily life. One can assume externally the behavior and discipline of the Hearer Vehicle; one can have the six perfections as explained in the Great Vehicle texts; then if in addition, one has the tantric practice of deity yoga, meditative stabilization (*samādhi, ting nge 'dzin*) will be achieved quickly and will become stable. Since this is the way Tibetans practice in daily life, I call these practices the "Treasures of Tibetan Buddhism."

COMPASSION IN
GLOBAL POLITICS

LOS ANGELES WORLD AFFAIRS COUNCIL, CALIFORNIA

THIS CENTURY is very sophisticated. Through various factors, mainly material, the world is becoming smaller and smaller, providing the peoples of the world with good opportunities to meet and talk with each other. Such contact provides a valuable chance to increase our understanding of each other's way of living, philosophy, and beliefs, and increased understanding will lead naturally to mutual respect. Because of the world's having become smaller, I have been able to come here today.

As we meet, I always keep in mind that we are the same in being human beings. If we emphasize the superficial differences, I am an Easterner and furthermore a Tibetan from beyond the Himalayas, with a different environment and a different culture. However, if we look deep down, I have a valid feeling of "I," and with that feeling, I want happiness and do not want suffering. Everyone, no matter where they are from, has this valid feeling of "I" on the conventional level, and in this sense we are all the same.

With this understanding as a basis, when I meet new people in new places, in my mind here is no barrier, no curtain. I can talk with you as I would to old friends even though this is the first time we meet. In my mind, as human beings you are my brothers and sisters; there is no difference in substance. I can express whatever I feel, without hesitation, just as to an old friend. With this feeling we can communicate without any difficulty and can contact heart to heart, not with just a few nice words, but really heart to heart.

Based on such genuine human relation—real feeling for each other, understanding each other—we can develop mutual trust and respect. From that, we can share other peoples' suffering and build harmony in human society. We can create a friendly human family.

This attitude is most useful. If we put too much emphasis on the superficial differences—culture, ideology, faith, race, color, wealth, and education—if we make small rigid discriminations, we cannot avoid making additional suffering for human society. A troublesome atmosphere will be created from these exaggerated but actually small differences.

Also, in world politics such small discriminations create uncontrollable problems. For instance, in Asia, the Middle East, Africa, or Latin America, strife comes sometimes from religious feelings, sometimes from race, sometimes from ideology. The same is true for my own country, Tibet, due to certain attitudes of our great neighbor, the People's Republic of China, that appeared during the Cultural Revolution. In this manner human ways of thinking create problems in addition to the basic ones that we must face.

For instance, although thousands upon thousands of refugees from Cambodia and Vietnam were dying, some people were talking about the politics of those refugees rather than handling the immediate problem properly. This is particularly saddening. That people in need are ignored for such reasons reveals what we are lacking—though we are intelligent and powerful, strong enough to exploit peoples or destroy the world, we lack real kindness and love. We need to realize right from the beginning that basically we are human beings who do not want to die and likewise these people are also human beings who do not want to die. They have the right to live as human beings; they need help.

First we must help; later we can talk about the causes, the politics that led to their tragedy, and so forth. There is an Indian saying: If you are struck by a poisonous arrow, it is important first to pull it out; there is no time to ask who shot it, what sort of poison it is, and so on. First handle the immediate problem, and later we can investigate. Similarly when we encounter human suffering, it is important to respond with compassion rather than to question the politics of those we help. Instead of asking whether their country is enemy or friend, we must think, "These are human beings, they are suffering, and they have a right to happiness equal to our own."

We are not lacking in terms of the development of science and technology; still, we lack something here in the heart—real inner warm feeling. A good heart is needed.

With the basic understanding of all humans as brothers and sisters, we can appreciate the usefulness of different systems and ideologies that can accommodate different individuals and groups that have different dispositions, different tastes. For certain people under certain conditions, a certain ideology or cultural heritage is more useful. Each person has the right to choose whatever is most suitable. This is the individual's business on the basis of deep understanding of all other persons as brothers and sisters.

Deep down we must have real affection for each other, a clear realization or recognition of our shared human status. At the same time, we must openly accept all ideologies and systems as means of solving humanity's problems. One country, one nation, one ideology, one system is not sufficient. It is helpful to have a variety of different approaches on the basis of a deep feeling of the basic sameness of humanity. We can then make joint effort to solve the problems of the whole of humankind. The problems human society is facing in terms of economic development, the crisis of energy, the tension between the poor and rich nations, and many geopolitical problems can be solved if we understand each others' fundamental humanity, respect each others' rights, share each others' problems and sufferings, and then make joint effort.

Even if we cannot solve certain problems, we should not regret it. We humans must face death, old age, and disease as well as natural disasters, such as hurricanes, that are beyond our control. We must face them; we cannot avoid them. But these sufferings are quite sufficient for us—why should we create other problems due to our own ideology, just differing ways of thinking? Useless! It is sad. Thousands upon thousands of people suffer from this. Such a situation is truly silly since we can avoid it by adopting a different attitude, appreciating the basic humanity which ideologies are supposed to serve.

Four or five hundred years ago in this country the native Indians lived in small communities, more or less independently; even family by family, they were mostly independent. However, now there is no question that even nation to nation, continent to continent, we are heavily dependent on each other. For instance, thousands upon thousands of new cars are moving in the streets of New York, Washington, or here in Los Angeles, but without oil they cannot move. Though at the moment human beings are carried by cars, if that fuel is finished, the humans will have to carry these big cars.

Prosperity depends on other factors in other places. Whether we like it or not, this shows that we are interdependent. We can no longer exist in complete isolation. Unless we have real cooperation, harmony, and common effort, difficulties will be created. Since we must live together, why not do so with a positive attitude, a good mind? Why is it that instead we feel hatred for each other and bring more trouble to the world?

I am a religious person, and from my viewpoint all things first originate in the mind. Things and events depend heavily on motivation. A real sense of appreciation of humanity, compassion, and love are the key points. If we develop a good heart, then whether the field is science, agriculture, or politics, since motivation is so important, these will all improve. A good heart is both important and effective in daily life. If in a small family, even without children, the members have a warm heart to each other, a peaceful atmosphere will be created. However, if one of the persons feels angry, immediately the atmosphere in the house becomes tense. Despite good food or a nice television set, you will lose peace and calm. Thus, things depend more on the mind than on matter. Matter is important, we must have it, we must use it properly, but this century must combine a good brain—intelligence—with a good heart.

Everybody loves to talk about calm and peace whether in a family, national, or international context, but without inner peace how can we make real peace? World peace through hatred and force is impossible. Even in the case of individuals, there is no possibility to feel happiness through anger. If in a difficult situation one becomes disturbed internally, overwhelmed by mental discomfort, then external things will not help at all. However, if despite external difficulties or problems, internally one's attitude is of love, warmth, and kind-heartedness, then problems can be faced and accepted easily.

The human essence of good sense finds no room with anger. Anger, jealousy, impatience, and hatred are the real troublemakers; with them problems cannot be solved. Though one may have temporary success, ultimately one's hatred or anger will create further difficulties. With anger, all actions are swift. When we face problems with compassion, sincerely and with good motivation, it may take longer, but ultimately the solution is better, for there is far less chance of creating a new problem through the temporary "solution" of the present one.

Sometimes we look down on politics, criticizing it as dirty. However, if you look at it properly, politics in itself is not wrong. It is an instrument to serve human society. With good motivation—sincerity and honesty—politics becomes an instrument in the service of society. But when motivated by selfishness with hatred, anger, or jealousy, it becomes dirty.

This is true not only for politics but also for religion. If I speak about religion with selfish motives or with hatred, then though I am talking about religion, it is not useful because the feeling behind it is bad. Things depend on our own motivation. Through money or power you cannot solve all problems. The problem in the human heart must first be solved. Then, the other human-created problems will be solved naturally.

My opinion is that since everybody belongs to this world, we must try to adopt a good attitude worldwide, a good feeling for our fellow brothers and sisters. In my particular case, we Tibetans are carrying on a struggle for our rights. Some say that the Tibetan situation is rather political, but I feel it is not. We Tibetans have a unique and distinct cultural heritage just as the Chinese have. We do not hate the Chinese; we deeply respect the riches of Chinese culture which spans so many centuries. Though we have deep respect and are not anti-Chinese, we six million Tibetans have an equal right to maintain our own distinctive culture as long as we do not harm others. Materially we are backward, but in spiritual matters—in terms of the development of the mind—we are quite rich. We Tibetans are Buddhists, and the Buddhism that we practice is a rather complete form of Buddhism. Also, we have kept it active, very much alive.

In the past century we remained a peaceful nation with our unique culture. Now, unfortunately, during the last few decades, this nation and culture are being deliberately destroyed. We like our own culture, our own land; we have the right to preserve it.

Also, the six million Tibetan people are human beings, no matter whether we are a materially backward country or not. We are six million human souls with the right to live as human beings. This is the problem.

I am serving our cause with the motivation of service to humankind, not for political reasons, not out of hatred. Not just as a Tibetan but as a human being, I think it is worthwhile to preserve that culture to contribute to world society. This is why I am persisting in our movement, and though some people see this as a purely political matter, I know it is not.

We hope very much that the over-all attitude of the People's Republic of China is changing, but we are cautious due to our past experience. I do not say this out of wish to criticize; rather, it is a fact. Upon investigation you can determine whether it is fact or not; time will tell.

I believe that human determination and will power are quite sufficient to challenge outside pressure and aggression. No matter how strong the evil force is, the flame of truth will not diminish. This is my belief.

As a friend, my request and wish is that individually and as an organization you try to promote a sense of brotherhood and sisterhood. We must promote compassion and love; this is our real duty. Government has too much business to have time for these things. As private persons we have more time to think along these lines—how to make a contribution to human society by promoting the development of compassion and a real sense of community.

In conclusion, no doubt you feel I am talking of an impractical dream. However, we human beings have a developed brain and limitless potential. Since even wild animals can gradually be trained with patience, the human mind also can gradually be trained, step by step. If you test these practices with patience, you can come to know this through your own experience. If someone who easily gets angry tries to control his or her anger, in time it can be controlled. The same is true for a selfish person; first that person must realize the faults of a selfish motivation and the benefit in being less selfish. Having realized this, one trains in it, trying to control the bad side and develop the good. As time goes by, such practice can be effective. This is the only alternative.

Without love, human society is in a very difficult state; without love, in the future we will face tremendous problems. Love is the center of human life.

MEDITATION

I AM VERY HAPPY to have come to your center. I know something about the activities here and admire your views and aims of close understanding of many systems. My thought is to explain something briefly and roughly at first, and then we can have an informal discussion.

If you ask, "Do humans have rights?," yes, there are human rights. How is it that humans have rights? It is on the basis of the valid innate appearance of an "I" to our consciousness that we naturally want happiness and do not want suffering, and that wanting of happiness and not wanting of suffering itself, with this appearance as its basis, is the very reason for there being human rights.

There are many levels of the happiness to be accomplished and the suffering to be relieved. Millions and millions of people in this world are seeking a path to gain happiness and remove suffering, considering their own to be the best method. All the big schemes for worldly development—the five year plans and ten year plans—arise in dependence on the wish for happiness. We who are gathered here today are seeking a means different from the usual to achieve happiness and remove suffering. We are mainly concerned with techniques based not on money but on the internal transformation of thought.

Many wise persons in the past set forth techniques for changing, training, and transforming the mind, and it is most important for us to have respect for all of these systems as being altruistically oriented and having a common aim. Respecting these various systems, one studies them to discover their unique techniques and to discover which are the most helpful and appropriate for oneself in order to practice them. We must implement them; these teachings are of little value unless they are put into practice in our daily lives.

The tenets of philosophical systems are to be practiced on the basis of a disciplined mental continuum; therefore, meditation is most important both in general and especially in the beginning. Perhaps today as I explain this topic, we could engage in an experiment. Would you like to participate? First, look to your posture: arrange your legs in the most comfortable position; set the backbone as straight as an arrow. Place your hands in the position of meditative equipoise, four finger widths below the navel, with the left hand on the bottom, right hand on top, and your thumbs touching to form a triangle. This placement of the hands has connection with the place inside the body where inner heat is generated.

Bending the neck down slightly, allow the mouth and teeth to be as usual, with the top of the tongue touching the roof of the mouth near the top teeth. Let the eyes gaze downwards loosely— it is not necessary that they be directed to the end of the nose; they can be pointed toward the floor in front of you if this seems more natural. Do not open the eyes too wide nor forcefully close them; leave them open a little. Sometimes they will close of their own accord; that is all right. Even if your eyes are open, when your mental consciousness becomes steady upon its object, these appearances to the eye consciousness will not disturb you.

For those of you who wear eye glasses, have you noticed that when you take off your glasses, because of the unclarity there is less danger from the generation of excitement and more danger of laxity? Do you find that there is a difference between facing and not facing the wall? When you face the wall, you may find that there is less danger of excitement or scattering. These kinds of things can be determined through your own experience.

Within meditations that have an object of observation, there can be two types of objects: external or internal. Now, instead of meditating on the mind itself, let us meditate on an external object of observation. For instance, the body of a Buddha for those who like to look at a Buddha or a cross for those who like that, or whatever symbol is suitable for you. Mentally visualize that the object is about four feet in front of you, at the same height as the eyebrows. The object should be approximately two inches high and emanating light. Try to conceive of it as being heavy, for this will prevent excitement. Its brilliance will prevent laxity. As you concentrate, you must strive for two factors: first, to make the object of observation clear and, second, to make it steady.

Has something appeared to your mind? Are the sense objects in front of your eyes bothering you? If that is the case, it is all right to close them, but with the eyes closed, do you see a reddish appearance? If you see red with the eyes closed or if you are bothered by what you see when your eyes are open, you are too involved with the eye consciousness and thus should try to withdraw attention from the eye consciousness and put it with the mental consciousness.

That which interferes with the steadiness of the object of observation and causes it to fluctuate is excitement or, in a more general way, scattering. To stop that, withdraw your mind more strongly inside so that the intensity of the mode of apprehension begins to lower. To withdraw the mind, it helps to think about something that makes you more sober, a little bit sad. These thoughts can cause your heightened mode of apprehension of the object, the mind's being too tight, to lower or loosen somewhat whereby you are better able to stay on the object of observation.

It is not sufficient just to have stability. It is necessary also to have clarity. That which prevents clarity is laxity, and what causes laxity is an over-withdrawal, excessive declination, of the mind. First of all, the mind becomes lax; this can lead to lethargy in which, losing the object of observation, you have as if fallen into darkness. This can lead even to sleep. When this occurs, it is necessary to raise or heighten the mode of apprehension. As a technique for that, think of something that you like, something that makes you joyous, or go to a high place or where there is a vast view. This technique causes the deflated mind to heighten in its mode of apprehension.

It is necessary within your own experience to recognize when the mode of apprehension has become too excited or too lax and determine the best practice for lowering or heightening it.

The object of observation that you are visualizing has to be held with mindfulness. Then, along with this, you inspect, as if from a corner, to see whether the object is clear and stable; the faculty that engages in this inspection is called introspection. When powerful steady mindfulness is achieved, introspection is generated, but the uncommon function of introspection is to inspect from time to time to see whether the mind has come under the influence of excitement or laxity. When you develop mindfulness and introspection well, you are able to catch laxity and excitement just before they arise and prevent their arising.

Briefly, that is how to sustain meditation with an external object of observation. Another type of meditation involves looking at the mind itself. Try to leave your mind vividly in a natural state, without thinking of what happened in the past or of what you are planning for the future, without generating any conceptuality.

Where does it seem that your consciousness is? Is it with the eyes or where is it? Most likely you have a sense that it is associated with the eyes since we derive most of our awareness of the world through vision. This is due to having relied too much on our sense consciousnesses. However, the existence of a separate mental consciousness can be ascertained; for example, when attention is diverted by sound, that which appears to the eye consciousness is not noticed. This indicates that a separate mental consciousness is paying more attention to sound heard by the ear consciousness than to the perceptions of the eye consciousness.

With consistent practice, consciousness may eventually be perceived or felt as an entity of mere luminosity and knowing, to which anything is capable of appearing and which, when appropriate conditions arise, can be generated in the image of whatsoever object. As long as the mind does not encounter the external circumstance of conceptuality, it will abide empty without anything appearing in it, like clear water. Its very entity is that of mere experience. In realizing this nature of the mind, we have for the first time located the object of observation of this internal type of meditation. The best time for practicing this form of meditation is in the morning, in a quiet place, when the mind is clear and alert.

There is yet another method of meditation that enables one to discern the ultimate nature of phenomena. Generally, phenomena are divided into two types: the mental and physical aggregates— or phenomena that are used by the "I"—and the "I" that uses them. To determine the nature of this "I," let us use an example. When we say John is coming, there is some person who is the one designated by the name John. Is this name designated to his body? It is not. Is it designated to his mind? If it were designated to his mind, we could not speak of John's mind. Mind and body are things used by the person. It almost seems that there is an "I" separate from mind and body. For instance, when we think, "Oh, my lousy body!" or "My lousy mind!," to our own innate mode of appearance the mind itself is not the "I," right? Now, what John is there who is not his mind or body? You also should apply this to yourself, to your own sense of "I"—where is this "I" in terms of mind and body?

When my body is sick, though my body is not "I," due to the body's being sick it can be posited that I am sick. In fact, for the sake of the well-being and pleasure of the "I," it sometimes even becomes necessary to cut off part of the body. Although the body is not the "I," there is a relationship between the two; the pain of the body can serve as the pain of the "I." Similarly, when the eye consciousness sees something, it appears to the mind that the "I" perceives it.

What is the nature of the "I"? How does it appear to you? When you do not fabricate or create any artificial concept in your mind, does it seem that your "I" has an identity separate from your mind and body? But if you search for it, can you find it? For instance, someone accuses you, "You stole this," or "You ruined such and such," and you feel, "I didn't do that!" At that time, how does the "I" appear? Does it appear as if solid? Does some solid, steady, and strong thing appear to your mind when you think or say, "I didn't do that!"

This seemingly solid, concrete, independent, self-instituting "I" under its own power that appears at such a time actually does not exist at all, and this specific non-existence is what is meant by the selflessness of the person. In the absence of analysis and investigation, a mere "I" as in, "I want such and such," or "I am going to do such and such," is asserted as valid, but the non-existence of an independent or self-powered "I" constitutes the selflessness of the person. This selflessness is what is found when one searches analytically to try to find the "I."

Such absence of inherent existence of the "I" is an ultimate truth, a final truth. The "I" that appears to a non-analytical conventional awareness is the dependently arisen "I" serving as the basis of the conventions of action, agent, and so forth; it is a conventional truth. In analyzing the mode of subsistence or the status of the "I," it is clear that although it appears to exist inherently, it does not, much like an illusion.

That is how the ultimate nature of the "I"—emptiness—is analyzed. Just as the "I" has this nature, so all other phenomena that are used by the "I" are empty of inherent existence. When analyzed, they cannot be found at all, but without analysis and investigation, they do exist. Their nature is the same as the "I."

The conventional existence of the "I" as well as of pleasure and pain make it necessary to generate compassion and altruism, and because the ultimate nature of all phenomena is this emptiness of inherent existence, it is also necessary to cultivate wisdom. When these two aspects—compassion and wisdom—are practiced in union, wisdom grows more profound, and the sense of duality diminishes. Due to the mind's dwelling in the meaning of emptiness, dualistic appearance becomes lighter, and at the same time the mind itself becomes more subtle. As the mind grows even more subtle, reaching the subtlest level, it is eventually transformed into the most basic mind, the fundamental innate mind of clear light, which at once realizes and is of one taste with emptiness, in meditative equipoise without any dualistic appearance at all, mixed with emptiness. Within all having this one taste, anything and everything can appear; this is known as "All in one taste, one taste in all."

Now perhaps we could have a discussion. Do you have any questions?

Question: Why is it better to meditate in the morning?

Answer: There are two main reasons. Physically, in the early morning—once you are used to it—all the nerve centers are fresh, and this is beneficial. Also, there is a difference just in terms of the time. If you have slept well, you are more fresh and alert in the morning; this we can see in our own experience. At night I reach a point where I cannot think properly; however, after sleeping and then waking in the early morning, that thing, which yesterday I could not properly think through, automatically appears more clearly. This shows that mental power is much sharper in the morning.

Question: Can you say something about meditation upon mantra as sound?

Answer: With regard to mantras that one can observe in meditation, there are external sounds of oral repetition and internal sounds of mental repetition. There are also natural self-arisen sounds, such as the appearance of the inhalation and exhalation of breath as the tones of mantra.

One can set the form of the letters standing on the edge of a flat moon-disc facing inward or within light at the heart. If it is comfortable for you to do so, imagine that you are in the middle of this, like in the house of your body. If you have a sense of the main part of consciousness being around the eyes, it is possible to imagine light behind the eyes and then, strongly identifying yourself as being there in the middle of that light, move the light and consciousness down to the center of the mantra circle which is at the heart. If you do this many times, you will gradually have the sense that you are right here in the heart. Then, with you in the center of the mantra, it can be as if you are reading the letters of the mantra around you, not orally but mentally—reciting mantra but not with the mouth. There are many different techniques.

Question: What is the most expedient means for overcoming resistance to meditation?

Answer: Five faults are explained as obstacles to meditation. The first is laziness; second is to forget the advice on the object, that is, to forget the object; next are laxity and excitement; then failure to apply an antidote when laxity or excitement are present, and the last is to continue applying the antidotes when laxity or excitement have already been overcome. These are called the five faults. Eight antidotes are explained for them. The antidotes to laziness are, first of all, the faith that intelligently sees the value of meditative stabilization, the prime value being that without it the higher paths cannot be generated. In dependence upon ascertaining the good qualities of meditative stabilization, aspiration seeking to attain those qualities is induced. By means of that, exertion comes, whereby you eventually attain pliancy causing body and mind to be free from unfavorable states and to be serviceable in a virtuous direction such that whatever virtue is done is powerful. These four are the antidotes to the first fault, laziness.

It is helpful not to practice too long in the beginning; do not over-extend yourself; the maximum period is around fifteen minutes. The important thing is not the length of the session but the quality of it. If you meditate too long, you can become sleepy, and then your meditation will become a matter of becoming accustomed to that state. This is not only a waste of time but also a habit that is difficult to eliminate in the future. In the beginning, start with many short sessions—even eight or sixteen sessions in a day—and then as you get used to the processes of meditation, the quality will improve, and the session will naturally become longer.

A sign that your meditative stabilization is progressing well is that even though your meditative session may be long, it will feel as though only a short time has passed. If it seems that you have spent a long time in meditation even though you have spent only a little, this is a sign that you should shorten the length of the session. This can be crucial at the beginning.

Question: Within the Buddhist system, they speak of different levels of cognition for which there are appropriate objects. On each level, who is the knower of these different modes of cognition?

Answer: There are many levels of consciousness, having different modes of perceiving objects, but they are all the same in being of a continuum of luminosity and knowing and in the fact that the mere "I" which is designated in dependence upon the continuum of consciousness is what knows them. Does that answer your question?

Among the various Buddhist systems, some posit types of consciousness as the "I" itself. However, in the highest, most profound system, the Middle Way Consequence School, that which is posited as the "I" is the mere "I" designated in dependence upon the continuum of consciousness.

Question: What is the distinction between consciousness and the "I"?

Answer: There are many different ways in which the "I" appears. One is for the "I" to appear to be factually different from the aggregates of mind and body and to be permanent, unitary, and under its own power. Another is for the "I," within not appearing to be factually other than the aggregates, to appear to be the bearer of the burden of the aggregates or the master of them—a substantially existent or self-sufficient "I." Then, another way is for the "I" to appear to be not posited through appearing to an awareness but to be established from the side of its own uncommon mode of subsistence. Then, another is for the "I" to appear to be inherently existent or existent in its own right, not seeming to exist through the force of nominality. Then, there is another in which, even though the "I" appears to exist in its own right, a mere "I" is all that is conceived. The conception of this last one is the only valid cognition among these.

What is the "I"? When it is sought analytically, it cannot be found. Nothing from among the mental and physical aggregates, nor the continuum of them, nor their collection can be posited as something that is the "I." When a speckled coil of rope in the dark appears to you to be a snake due to the darkness of its location, the parts of the rope individually, the parts of the rope together, or the continuum of those parts over time—none of these—can be posited as a snake. The snake exists only through the force of the mind of the fearful person; from the side of the rope there is nothing that is established as a snake.

As in that example, nothing among the mental and physical aggregates that are the basis of designation of the "I," either separately or together or as their continuum over time, can be posited as something that is the "I." Also, it is completely impossible to find the "I" as a factuality separate from the mind and body that are the basis of designation of "I." Now, if you began to think that therefore the "I" does not exist at all, this would be damaged by conventional valid cognition. The fact that the "I" exists is obvious.

The existence of the "I" is certified by experience, by valid cognition, but it is unfindable among its bases of designation. Thus, the "I" only designatedly exists through the force of nominality or conceptuality, through a subjective force. On what does it nominally depend? Its mere nominal existence is posited in dependence upon its basis of designation.

With regard to the mental and physical aggregates that are its basis of designation and among which there are many grosser and subtler levels, the subtlest is the beginningless consciousness that goes throughout all lifetimes. Therefore, it is said that the "I" is designated through the power of nominality in dependence upon the beginningless and endless continuum of consciousness, the main basis of designation. The "I" merely exists nominally, designated in dependence upon this continuum of consciousness. The conclusion is that except for a self that exists through the power of nominality, there is no self, no self that is established from its own side. This lack of establishment in the object's own right is the meaning of selflessness.

You might ask, "If the 'I' and so forth exist through the power of conceptuality, through whose conceptuality are these designated—mine, yours, one in the past, present, or whatever?" This again is a case of analyzing to try to find the object designated, and you will not find such. Therefore, existence through the force of conceptuality itself exists only through the force of conceptuality. Buddha said that all phenomena are only nominal and that mere nominality itself is only nominal. Emptiness itself is empty. Even Buddha is empty of inherent existence. Through emptiness the extreme of the reification of existence is avoided, but through the fact that things are not utterly non-existent and instead are dependent-arisings the extreme of utter non-existence is avoided.

Question: From where does consciousness arise?

Answer: We say that consciousness is produced from consciousness. Consciousness must be produced from consciousness because it cannot be produced with matter as its substantial cause. Particles cannot create an entity of luminosity and knowing. Matter cannot be the substantial cause of consciousness, and consciousness cannot be the substantial cause of matter. Although in the Mind-Only School matter is asserted as of the same entity as consciousness—almost as if there is nothing except consciousness, this is not asserted in the Middle Way Consequence School because such is damaged by reasoning. In this school, consciousness and matter are posited separately.

There is no way to posit consciousness except as being a continuation of former moments of consciousness; in this way consciousness can have no beginning, in which case rebirths can have no beginning. The mind in general has no beginning; the continuation of it has no beginning or end, but there are specific minds that have a beginning but no end and others that have no beginning but an end.

Question: My question is in regard to the two truths. Conventional truths presuppose the inherent existence of subject and object, and ultimate truth means the absence of inherent existence of subject and object. This seems clear, but when it is asserted that a conventional truth is not different from ultimate truth, I find this difficult to understand.

Answer: The Consequence School does not accept that subject and object inherently exist even conventionally. Due to misinterpretation of the view of the Consequence School, the lower systems say that therefore the Consequentialists have fallen into the extreme of nihilism; this indicates that even in their sight the Consequence School does not assert inherent existence even conventionally.

We do not say that the two truths are one, but that they are of one entity. They are, in fact, mutually exclusive. For instance, the back and front of the hand are of one hand, but the front and back of one hand are mutually exclusive. Similarly, when the conventionally existent "I" is asserted as the basis or substratum and its emptiness of inherent existence is posited as its mode of subsistence, this emptiness of inherent existence is the nature, basic disposition, and an attribute of the "I," and the "I" is its substratum or basis. There is one entity of the mere "I" and its emptiness, but the "I" is found by conventional valid cognition, whereas its emptiness is found by ultimate valid cognition, and thus the "I" and its emptiness are mutually exclusive—the one is not the other. Therefore, the two truths are one entity within being, technically speaking, different isolatable factors.

The main reason why the "I" or any other phenomenon is empty is because it is a dependent-arising. Dependent and independent are a dichotomy; when one is eliminated, the other is established. For instance, consider human and non-human: when something is established as one of these, it is eliminated that it is the other, and vice versa. When it is determined with respect to a specific phenomenon whether it is dependent or independent, in deciding that it is dependent, there is also an emptiness of independence with it, and that is what we call "emptiness of inherent existence." Also, when something is proved to be empty by the fact that it is a dependent arising, then it is within being existent that it is dependent. The non-existent cannot be dependent.

When you have become familiar with the reasoning of dependent-arising, the mere fact that something exists is sufficient reason for its being empty of inherent existence. However, since in most systems the fact that something exists is taken to indicate that it exists from its own side and is not empty of inherent existence, we use the reasoning of dependent-arising, reflecting on its implications.

Question: Could you please say something about the meditational Buddhas?

Answer: These are the Buddhas of the five lineages. They are explained in terms of the five constituents, the five aggregates, the five afflictive emotions, and the five wisdoms of the ordinary state. Let us consider the five constituents that are included within a person's continuum: earth, water, fire, wind, and space. These five constituents are the bases of purification to be purified into the five Buddha lineages. With respect to the form aggregate, when we die, this coarse body does not continue with us, but there is a subtler form aggregate that continues in the intermediate state through to the next life. Thus, if we consider the form aggregate without making a distinction between coarse and subtle, we can speak of a beginningless and endless continuum of the form aggregate. The purified aspect of this form aggregate is called Vairochana.

Consciousness is divided into minds and mental factors. There are six minds and fifty-one mental factors. One group of mental factors comprises the five omnipresent factors, among which one is feeling. This is the feeling aggregate. The purified form of the feeling aggregate is Ratnasambhava.

The purified aspect of the aggregate of discriminations is Amitābha; the aggregate of compositional factors, in its purified form, is Amoghasiddhi. Finally, the purified aspect of the aggregate of main consciousness is Akṣhobhya.

Whereas the five aggregates can be divided into gross and subtle forms, the five Buddha lineages apply to the subtler aggregates which have existed beginninglessly.

Question: Are the subtler aggregates equivalent to the Buddhas of the five lineages?

Answer: The five subtler aggregates will eventually be transformed into the Buddhas of the five lineages. They are now as if accompanied by mental defilements. When the defilements are removed, these factors do not become any coarser or subtler; their nature remains, but due to having become separated from the faults of mental pollution, they have become the Buddhas of the five lineages. So if you ask whether the Buddhas of the five lineages are present now in our continuums, these factors are currently bound by faults and since there cannot be a Buddha who has a fault, they are not Buddhas. One is not yet fully enlightened, but that which is going to become a Buddha is present; therefore, these factors presently existent in our continuums are Buddha seeds and are called the Buddha nature or the matrix-of-One-Gone-Thus (*tathāgatagarbha, de bzhin gshegs pa'i snying po*).

More specifically, if you consider just the subtlest mind and the wind, or energy, that serves as its mount, the mere factor of luminosity and knowing of the subtlest mind itself as well as the energy associated with it are what will be transformed into the mind and body of a Buddha. This is the mind that will turn into an omniscient consciousness—a Buddha's mind; it is this mind that will be transformed, not some other mind coming from the outside. In other words, the Buddha nature is inherent; it is not imported from somewhere else.

This is true because the very entity of the mind, its nature of mere luminosity and knowing, is not polluted by defilements; they do not abide in the entity of the mind. Even when we generate afflictive emotions, the very entity or nature of the mind is still mere luminosity and knowing, and because of this we are able to remove the afflictive emotions.

It is suitable to think that the Buddhas of the five lineages of the ordinary state exist in us now, just as we speak of the three Buddha bodies of the ordinary state as being with us now. But it is not appropriate to speak of Buddhas, stainless and enlightened, rid of all faults and possessing all good qualities, as being in us now. If you agitate the water in a pond, it becomes cloudy with mud;

yet the very nature of the water itself is not dirty. When you allow it to become still again, the mud will settle, leaving the water pure.

How are the defilements removed? They are not removed by outside action nor by leaving them as they are; they are removed by the power of antidotes, meditative remedies. To understand this, take the example of anger. All anger is impelled and polluted by improper conceptuality. When we are angry at someone, what is that person like? How does he or she appear to your mind? How are you apprehending the person? That person appears to be self-instituted under his or her own power, and we apprehend the person as something really solid and forceful. And at the same time our own feelings appear equally substantial.

Both the object of our anger and subject, oneself, appear to exist concretely, as if established by way of their own character. Both seem forcefully to exist in their own right. But as I was saying earlier, things do not actually exist in this concrete way. As much as we are able to see the absence of inherent existence, that much will our conception of inherent existence and its assistance to anger be lessened.

The sign that our perceptions are superimposing a goodness or badness beyond what is actually present is that while desirous or angry we feel that the object is terrifically good or bad but afterwards when we think about the experience, it is laughable that we viewed the object that way; we understand that our perception was not true. These afflicted consciousnesses do not have any valid support. The mind which analytically searches for the inherent existence of an object finds ascertainment of its absence of inherent existence through valid reasoning, and thus this kind of consciousness does have a valid foundation. Like a debate in court, one perception is based on reason and truth, while the other one is not. When the evidence is sufficient, in such a debate the true view eventually overpowers the other because it can withstand analysis.

It is impossible for the mind simultaneously to apprehend one object in contradictory ways. With respect to one object, therefore, as you get used to understanding its absence of inherent existence, not only is it impossible at that time to generate a conception of inherent existence but also as strong as the correct realization becomes, so much, in general, does conception of its opposite weaken in force.

To generate such wisdom we engage in meditation because our minds, as they are now, are not powerful. Our mind is presently scattered; its energies need to be channeled like the way water in a hydroelectric plant is channeled to create great force. We achieve this with the mind through meditation, channeling it such that it becomes forceful, at which point it can be utilized in the direction of wisdom. Since all the substances for enlightenment exist within ourselves, we should not look for Buddhahood somewhere else.

With respect to purifying the afflictive emotions, it is in terms of this basic entity of an angry consciousness—mere luminosity and knowing—that it is purified into Akṣhobhya. As I said earlier, even when we generate an afflictive emotion, it does not pollute the nature of the mind, and it itself is pervaded by the factor of luminosity and knowing. Hatred is itself a consciousness, because of which it has a nature of mere luminosity and knowing, even though it conceives its object in an incorrect manner.

Thus, the substances that can turn into Buddhahood are with us now, but not actual Buddhahood. If you felt that Buddhahood must be here now just because its causes are, you would incur the fault that Dharmakīrti demonstrates to such an assertion—that on the top of a single blade of grass where a small worm is staying there are the hundred elephants as which that worm will take rebirth in the future due to karma that is already in its continuum. There is the difference, however, that the seeds for being reborn as an elephant are newly accumulated through actions,

Surrounded by a sea of cameras on his arrival at Kennedy Airport, New York. Photo: N. Vreeland

Among his first appearances on network television was this late-night interview with Tom Snyder. Photo: N. Vreeland

His Holiness resting in his suite at the Waldorf-Astoria.
Photo: N. Vreeland

Introduced by Whitney North Seymour of Freedom House, at the first press conference held in the U.S. Photo: N. Vreeland

Luncheon meeting with representatives from Newsweek, The New York Times, *and other publications. Photo: N. Vreeland*

*Greeting an elderly Kalmyk Mongolian at the Lamaist Buddhist
Monastery. Photo:A. Djambinov*

*Geshe Wangyal of the Lamaist Buddhist Monastery, Washington,
New Jersey. Photo:A. Djambinov*

Cardinal Cooke and Mayor Ed Koch hold traditional white scarves presented at St. Patrick's Cathedral. Photo: A. Djambinov

A meeting with His Holiness Dudjom Rinpoche, Orgyen Chö Dzong, New York City. Photo: J. Andersson

Teaching given to a Buddhist group in California. Photo: J. Andersson

On the steps of the Lincoln Memorial, Washington, D.C.
Photo: N. Vreeland

A gathering of the Council on Religious and International Affairs,
Merrill House, New York City. Photo: N. Vreeland

With Anthony Damiani, Director of Wisdom's Goldenrod, Center for Philosophical Studies, Ithaca, New York. Photo: M. Loveland

*One of several meetings with various Congressional committees,
Washington, D.C.* Photo: J. Andersson

Visiting the Jefferson Memorial, Washington, D.C. Photo: N. Vreeland

At a Congressional reception, Washington, D.C.   Photo: A. Djambinov

*With Chogyam Trungpa Rinpoche, New York Dharmadhatu,
New York City.   Photo: J. Andersson*

Addressing the Asia Society at Central Presbyterian Church, New York City. Photo: N. Vreeland

Informally addressing students in Washington, New Jersey.
Photo: A. Djambinov

His Holiness the Fourteenth Dalai Lama, Charlottesville, Virginia.
Photo: N. Vreeland

whereas the seeds of the Buddhas of the five lineages subsist within us naturally.

Question: Do you associate the sun, or a solar deity, with any of the Buddhas of the five lineages?

Answer: Though your question is brief, it requires a detailed answer. The sun and moon deities in Buddhism are, so to speak, ordinary deities. To understand the levels, it is necessary to make a division of the three realms: the Desire, Form, and Formless Realms. In each of these realms there are different societies of gods. There are four main groups in the Formless Realm and seventeen in the Form Realm. Within the Desire Realm, there are two types: societies of gods and societies of beings who are not gods, such as humans. Of the gods in the Desire Realm, there are six types: the gods of the Four Great Royal Lineages, the Heaven of the Thirty-Three, Those Free From Combat, the Joyous, Those Enjoying Emanations, and Those Having Control Over Others' Emanations. The deities of the sun and moon probably are included within the gods in the Heaven of the Thirty-Three. All of these are still bound within cyclic existence.

Question: Could you please say something about the nature of mandalas?

Answer: Mandala, in general, means that which extracts the essence. There are many usages of the term mandala according to context. One type of mandala is the offering of the entire world system with the major and minor continents mentally made to high beings. Also, there are painted mandalas, mandalas of concentration, those made out of colored sand, mandalas of the conventional mind of enlightenment, mandalas of the ultimate mind of enlightenment, and so forth. Because one can extract a meaning from each of these through practicing them, they are all called mandalas.

Although we might call these pictures and constructed depictions mandalas, the main meaning is for oneself to enter into the mandala and extract an essence in the sense of receiving blessing. It is a place of gaining magnificence. Because one is gaining a blessing into magnificence and thereupon developing realizations, it is called an extraction or assumption of something essential.

Question: How does one choose a teacher or know a teacher to be reliable?

Answer: This should be done in accordance with your interest and disposition, but you should analyze well. You must investigate before accepting a lama or guru to see whether that person is really qualified or not. It is said in a scripture of the Discipline (*vinaya, 'dul ba*) that just as fish that are hidden under the water can be seen through the movement of ripples from above, so also a teacher's inner qualities can, over time, be seen a little through that person's behavior.

We need to look into the person's scholarship—the ability to explain topics—and whether the person implements those teachings in conduct and experience. A tantra says that you must investigate carefully even if it takes twelve years. This is the way to choose a teacher.

I like the fact that you think seriously about these matters and put forward serious questions. We can now have silence and meditation.

BUDDHISM EAST TO WEST

WE ARE GATHERED HERE today generally speaking because each of us is seeking a deeper meaning in life. In the past few days I have said many times that along with material progress, inner development is important and useful. You yourselves can observe that when persons who have inner strength face problems, they are better equipped to confront them. In the case of Tibet and my own experience, limited though it may be, I have found this to be true. Someone in my position, in a complicated situation and having large responsibilities may, under such circumstances, come to have some mental problems. However, as you may read from my face, I am not much bothered. Of course, we realize the very great problems, the tragedy; yet we accept them as facts and try our best. There is no doubt that an attitude of inner strength can help; it influences the way we approach and confront problems.

Since everyone has more or less the same nature, the practice of religion, in this case Buddhism, has something deep and useful for one's life. This is not necessarily to bring about a good rebirth, and so forth; even within this one life if we adopt a right attitude toward our fellow humans, that itself will give in return great satisfaction. The principles are good motivation and compassion.

Although compassion is explained mainly in the Bodhisattva

scriptures—the Great Vehicle—all Buddhist ideas are based on compassion. All of Buddha's teachings can be expressed in two sentences. The first is, "You must help others." This includes all the Great Vehicle teachings. "If not, you should not harm others." This encompasses the whole teaching of the Hearer Vehicle, or Theravādayāna. It expresses the basis of all ethics, which is to cease harming others. Both teachings are based on the thought of love, compassion. A Buddhist should, if possible, help others. If this is not possible, at least do not do any harm to others.

When we practice, initially, as a basis we control ourselves, stopping the bad actions that hurt others as much as we can. This is defensive. After that, when we develop certain qualifications, then as an active goal we should help others. In the first stage, sometimes we need isolation while pursuing our own inner development; however, after you have some confidence, some strength, you must remain with, contact, and serve society in any field—health, education, politics, or whatever.

There are people who call themselves religious-minded, trying to show this by dressing in a peculiar manner, maintaining a peculiar way of life, and isolating themselves from the rest of society. That is wrong. A scripture of mind-purification (mind-training) says, "Transform your inner viewpoint, but leave your external appearance as it is." This is important. Because the very purpose of practicing the Great Vehicle is service for others, you should not isolate yourselves from society. In order to serve, in order to help, you must remain in society.

That is one point. The second is that particularly in Buddhism while we practice we must use the brain as well as the heart. On the ethical side, we must practice the quality of a good and warm heart; also, since Buddhism is very much involved in reasoning and logic—the wisdom side—intelligence is important. Thus, a combination of mind and heart is needed. Without knowledge, without fully utilized intelligence, you cannot reach the depths of the Buddhist doctrine; it is difficult to achieve concrete or fully qualified wisdom. There may be exceptions, but this is the general rule.

It is necessary to have a combination of hearing, thinking, and meditating. The Kadampa (*bka' gdams pa*) teacher Dromtön (*'brom ston pa,* 1004-1064) said, "When I engage in hearing, I also make effort at thinking and meditating. When I engage in thinking, I also search out more hearing and engage in meditation. And when I meditate, I don't give up hearing and don't give up thinking." He said, "I am a balanced Kadampa," meaning that he maintained a balance of hearing, thinking, and meditating.

When engaging in hearing, it is important to mix the mind, to familiarize the mind, with what is being heard. The study of religion is not like learning about history. It must be mixed with your mental continuum; your mind should be suffused with it. A sūtra says that the practices are like a mirror; your actions of body, speech, and mind are like a face to be seen in the mirror; and through the practices you should recognize faults and gradually get rid of them. As it is said in the oral transmission, "If there is enough space between yourself and the practices for someone else to walk through, then you are not implementing them properly." In that case, the practices become something like an object of entertainment. And if it is that, it can turn into an object of argument. Then after a good deal of argument, it can even lead to fighting. This is not at all the purpose of religion.

While we are learning the practices, we must relate them to our own behavior. There is a story of a Kadampa scholar-yogi who was reading in the Discipline that it was not suitable to use an animal skin on one's seat; he was sitting on a bearskin, so he immediately pulled it out from under himself. Then as he read further, he learned that it was permissible to use such if the weather was cold or the person was sick, and so he carefully brought it back.

This is true practice—immediately to implement what you are learning.

If one is learning religion in general or Buddhism as an academic study, it is different right from the beginning. The motivation is just to acquire knowledge of another topic of learning. However, we who are supposed to be Buddhists, who are supposed to practice, should try to implement the teachings while we are learning. Then we can experience their real value.

The third point I would like to make is that when you start practicing, you should not expect too much. We live in a time of computers and automation, so you may feel that inner development is also an automatic thing for which you press a button and everything changes. It is not so. Inner development is not easy and will take time. External progress, the latest space missions and so forth, have not reached their present level within a short period but over centuries, each generation making greater developments based on those of the previous generation. However, inner development is even more difficult since internal improvement cannot be transferred from generation to generation. Your past life's experience very much influences this life, and this life's experience becomes the basis for the next rebirth's development, but transference of inner development from one person to another is impossible. Thus, everything depends on yourself, and it will take time.

I have met Westerners who at the beginning were enthusiastic about their practice, but after a few years have completely forgotten it, and there are no traces of what they had practiced at one time. This is because at the beginning they expected too much. Shāntideva's *Engaging in the Bodhisattva Deeds* emphasizes the importance of the practice of patience—tolerance. This tolerance is an attitude not only towards your enemy but also an attitude of sacrifice, of determination, so that you do not fall into the laziness of discouragement. You should practice patience with great resolve. This is important.

Let me use myself as an example. I was born into a Buddhist family in a country that is primarily Buddhist, although there are also Christians and Muslims as well as many followers of the ancient Tibetan religion, Bön. I was able to learn Buddhism in my native language and from a very young age became a monk. Thus, from the viewpoint of practicing the Buddhist doctrine, I had much more facility than you. But in terms of my own development, around fifteen or sixteen years of age I began to have real enthusiasm for practice. I have been practicing since then and now am forty-four. Looking back over those years, I can notice that there has been improvement over periods of two to three years. Within a few weeks, I can notice little. Thus determination to practice without loosening effort is important.

Inner development comes step by step. You may think, "Today my inner calmness, my mental peace, is very small," but still, if you compare, if you look five, ten, or fifteen years back, and think, "What was my way of thinking then? How much inner peace did I have then and what is it today?"—comparing it with what it was then, you can realize that there is some progress, there is some value. This is how you should compare—not with today's feeling and yesterday's feeling, or last week or last month, even not last year, but five years ago. Then you can realize what improvement has occurred internally. Progress comes by maintaining constant effort in daily practice.

People sometimes ask me whether Buddhism—an ancient teaching which comes from the East—is suitable for Westerners or not. My answer is that the essence of all religions deals with basic human problems. As long as human beings, whether from the north, south, east, or west—white, black, yellow, or red—have the sufferings of birth, disease, old age, and death, all are equal in that respect. As long as these basic human sufferings are there, since the essential teaching is concerned with that suffering, there is not much question whether it is suitable or not.

Still, there is a question with regard to each individual's mental disposition. Some people are more fond of one food; others find another more suitable. Similarly, for some individuals a certain religion brings more benefit whereas in other cases another brings more benefit. Under the circumstances, the variety of teachings found in human society is necessary and useful, and among Westerners, no doubt there are people who find Buddhism suitable to their requirements.

When we speak of the essence, there is no question about suitability and no need to change the basic doctrines. However, on the superficial level change is possible. A Burmese monk in the Theravāda tradition whom I met recently in Europe and for whom I developed great respect makes the distinction between cultural heritage and religion itself. I call this a distinction between the superficial ceremonial or ritual level and the essence of a religion. In India, Tibet, China, Japan, or wherever, the religious aspect of Buddhism is the same, but the cultural heritage is different in each country. Thus, in India, Buddhism incorporated Indian culture; in Tibet, Tibetan culture, and so on. From this viewpoint, the incorporation of Buddhism into Western and other cultures may also be possible.

The essence of the Buddhist teachings does not change; wherever it goes it is suitable; however, the superficial aspects—certain rituals and ceremonies—are not necessarily suitable for a new environment; those things will change. How they will change in a particular place we cannot say. This evolves over time. When Buddhism first came from India to Tibet, no one had the authority to say, "Now Buddhism has come to a new land; from now on we must practice it in this way or that way." There was no such decision. It gradually evolved, and in time a unique tradition arose. Such may be the case for Westerners; gradually, in time, there may be a Buddhism combined with Western culture. In any case, this generation—your generation—who are starting this new idea in new countries have a big responsibility to take the essence and adjust it to your own environment.

For this we must use the brain to investigate. You should not go to either extreme—too conservative is not good, too radical is also not good. As in our Middle Way theory, one should follow a middle course. It is important to keep a middle approach in every field. Even in our daily consumption of food, we must follow a moderate way. With too much in our stomachs, trouble will come to us; too little is not sufficient. So, in our daily life—in our whole way of life—it is important to remain in the middle; both extremes must be checked. This brain must have full knowledge about the environment and the cultural heritage—full knowledge about what sort of things are of value in day to day life and what things, though part of the cultural heritage, may not be useful in daily life.

In the case of Tibetan culture, for example, certain past traditions may not be useful in the future. When under new circumstances the social system and way of social thinking change, certain aspects of a culture may no longer be useful. In the same way, if in the United States and Canada there are some aspects of the old culture that are not useful in modern daily life, they should be modified, and other aspects that are still meaningful and useful should be retained. You should try to combine that culture and Buddhism.

If you really take an interest in Buddhism, then the most important thing is implementation—practice. To study Buddhism and then use it as a weapon in order to criticize others' theories or ideologies is wrong. The very purpose of religion is to control yourself, not to criticize others. Rather, we must criticize ourselves. How much am I doing about my anger? About my attachment, about my hatred, about my pride, my jealousy? These are the things that we must check in daily life with the knowledge of Buddhist teachings. Clear?

As Buddhists, while we practice our own teaching, we must respect other faiths, Christianity, Judaism, and so forth. We must recognize and appreciate their contributions over many past centuries to human society, and at this time we must strive to make common effort to serve humankind. The adopting of a right attitude toward other faiths is particularly important for new Buddhists to keep in mind.

Also among Buddhists, there are different schools, different systems of practice, and we should not feel that one teaching is better, another teaching is worse, and so on. Sectarian feeling and criticism of other teachings or other sects is very bad, poisonous, and should be avoided.

The most important thing is practice in daily life; then you can know gradually the true value of religion. Doctrine is not meant for mere knowledge but for the improvement of our minds. In order to do that, it must be part of our life. If you put religious doctrine in a building and when you leave the building depart from the practices, you cannot gain its value.

I hope that you engage in practice with a good heart and from that motivation contribute something good to Western society. That is my prayer and wish.

Question: How can one work with deep fears most effectively?

Answer: There are quite a number of methods. The first is to think about actions and their effects. Usually when something bad happens, we say, "Oh, very unlucky," and when something good happens, we say, "Oh, very lucky." Actually, these two words, lucky and unlucky, are insufficient. There must be some reason. Because of a reason, a certain time became lucky or unlucky, but usually we do not go beyond lucky or unlucky. The reason, according to the Buddhist explanation, is: our past karma, our actions.

One way to work with deep fears is to think that the fear comes as a result of your own actions in the past. Further, if you have fear of some pain or suffering, you should examine whether there is anything you can do about it. If you can, there is no need to worry about it; if you cannot do anything, then there is also no need to worry.

Another technique is to investigate who is becoming afraid. Examine the nature of your self. Where is this "I"? Who am "I"? What is the nature of "I"? Is there an "I" besides my physical body and my consciousness? This may help.

Also, someone who is engaging in the Bodhisattva practices seeks to take others' suffering onto himself or herself. When you have fear, you can think, "Others have fear similar to this; may I take to myself all of their fears." Even though you are opening yourself to greater suffering, taking greater suffering to yourself, your fear lessens.

Yet another way is not to let your mind stay with the thought of fear but to put it on something else and let the fear just become lost. That is just a temporary method. Also, if you have a sense of fear due to insecurity, you can imagine for instance, if you are lying down, that your head is in Buddha's lap. Sometimes this may help psychologically. Another method is to recite mantra.

Question: In this country men and women intermingle freely and since old values are no longer adhered to, there is much confusion about what is right conduct. How are male/female relationships to be a part of Buddhist practice?

Answer: There are various levels. Monks and nuns are to be celibate and those who cannot do that can be lay practitioners. The conduct of a householder is to abandon adultery. Further, there are divisions within those who are and are not married.

Question: Please speak on the subject of love and marriage.

Answer: I do not have much to say. My simple opinion is that making love is all right, but for marriage, don't hurry, be cautious. Make sure you will remain forever, at least for this whole life. That is important, for if you marry hurriedly without understanding well what you are doing, then after a month or after a year, trouble starts, and you will be seeking divorce. From a legal viewpoint, divorce is possible, and without children it may be acceptable, but with children, it is not. It is not sufficient that a couple think of only their own love affairs and their own pleasure. You have a moral responsibility to think of your children. If the parents divorce, the child is going to suffer, not just temporarily, but for his or her whole life. The model for a person is one's own parents. If the parents are always fighting and finally divorce, I think that unconsciously, deep down, the child is badly influenced, imprinted. This is a tragedy. Thus, my advice is that for real marriage, there is no hurry: proceed cautiously, and marry only after good understanding; then you will have a happy marriage. Happiness in the home will lead to happiness in the world.

The compassion and kindness that people have for each other can be of two types—one that is involved with afflictive emotions and one that is not. That not involved with afflictive emotions is such that when you investigate or examine it, it becomes steadier and steadier and clearer and clearer. Not matter how much time passes, it becomes more firm. But when it is mixed with afflictive emotions, it will be there for a day or two and then will not.

Question: I do not feel worthwhile as a person. How can I work on this as a beginning meditation student?

Answer: You should not be discouraged. Human potential is the same for all. Your feeling, "I am of no value," is wrong. Absolutely wrong. You are deceiving yourself. We all have the power of thought—so what are you lacking? If you have will power, then you can do anything. If you become discouraged, thinking, "How could such a person as me possibly do anything?," then there is no way you can succeed. Therefore, in Buddhism it is usually said that you are your own master. You can do anything.

Question: What is the role of the teacher in practice? Is it necessary to have a teacher?

Answer: Yes, but it depends on the subject. General subjects, general Buddhist ideas, can be learned through books without a teacher. But certain complicated subjects are difficult to understand by just reading books without an experienced person's instruction and explanation. Generally speaking, a teacher is needed.

Question: Your Holiness has spoken of service. How can we be of service in Western society?

Answer: If you help even only one person, that is help. There is great opportunity to help others in the field of education, in schools, colleges, and so forth. Many Christian brothers and sisters are carrying out such work which I admire very much and from which Buddhists must learn. So in the fields of education and health, you can give direct service.

Also in jobs such as working for a company or as a factory

worker, even though you may not be directly helping others, indirectly you are serving society. Even though you are doing it for the sake of your salary, indirectly it does help people, and you should do it with a good motivation, trying to think, "My work is meant to help people." If you were making guns or bullets, of course it would be difficult. If you are making bullets and all the time thinking, "I am doing this to help others," it would be hypocritical, wouldn't it?

Question: Can one attain enlightenment without separating from the world?

Answer: Certainly. To renounce the world means to give up your attachment to the world. It does not mean that you have to separate yourself from it. The very purpose of the Buddhist doctrine is to serve others. In order to serve others you must remain in society. You should not isolate yourself from the rest of society.

Question: On your journey through this country so far, are there any surprising or particularly interesting things that stand out? I am curious about your general impressions of our country.

Answer: No particular surprise. Certainly this is a great country. I think it is quite liberal with respect to different ideas and different traditions. That is good. I find the people generally open and straightforward; I like this.

DEITIES

EXHIBITIONS like this one on Tibet are helpful for introducing people to a culture. We Tibetans have a distinctive culture. Materially, we are rather poor, but in spiritual and cultural development we are quite rich with much to offer the world. For instance, from my own experience I know that the Tibetan medical system is particularly valuable, especially for a number of chronic diseases. In fact, because of its usefulness, despite the deliberate destruction of Tibetan culture by the Chinese, they have left the Tibetan medical system intact and have even preserved and promoted it.

The objects of a culture represent that culture in part, but the main part of a culture is not in paintings and so forth but inside the mind. If it is alive in the daily life of people, we can know its usefulness. For instance, because of Tibetan culture, Tibetans for the most part are jovial people. We ourselves had not noticed it, but many foreigners who visited India noticed our joviality and asked what our "secret" is. Gradually, I came to think that it is due to our Buddhist culture that emphasizes the Bodhisattva ideal of compassion in a great many ways. Whether literate or illiterate, we are accustomed to hearing and speaking of all sentient beings as mothers and fathers. Even someone who looks like a ruffian has "all mothers, all sentient beings" on his lips. I feel that this ideal is the cause of our happiness. It is particularly helpful in daily life when facing serious problems.

However, perhaps you may wonder why we Tibetans keep talking about compassion and yet some of our deities are so fierce. Let me explain this.

In general, in Buddhism gods or deities are divided into two types, mundane and supramundane. Within the mundane, there are descriptions of many types of gods and demi-gods included within the six types of transmigrating beings—hell-beings, hungry ghosts, animals, humans, demi-gods, and gods. In the Desire Realm there are six types of gods; in the Form Realm there are four types corresponding to the four concentrations which are further divided into seventeen types; and in the Formless Realm there are four. Then, there are bad spirits that are included within hungry ghosts, demi-gods, and animals. There are many different types of spirits which I will not detail here.

Because there are many societies of gods, it is important to make a distinction between mundane and supramundane deities; otherwise, you could mistake a local, mundane deity for a supramundane deity of Highest Yoga Tantra, for instance. There are mundane deities that take possession of people and use them as mediums, but these beings are like us in that they have the afflictive emotions of desire and hatred. In the course of our lives, we have been born as such beings, and they have been born like us. From the Buddhist viewpoint, beings have limitless different types of good and bad karma due to which they come to appear in limitless different ways.

With respect to supramundane deities, there are two main types: those who are Bodhisattvas, who have attained the path of seeing the truth, and those who are Buddhas. Among those who appear as Bodhisattvas, there are two types: those who are actually Buddhas but appear as Bodhisattvas and those who are actually

Bodhisattvas. Among those who are Buddhas and Bodhisattvas, there are many who appear as protectors such as Mahākāla, Mahākālī, and so forth.

Deities in mandalas are supramundane ones who have reached the path of no more learning and are Buddhas. In Yoga Tantra, for instance, there are mandalas with even a thousand deities who are appearances of the one central deity. In a Highest Yoga Tantra mandala of Guhyasamāja there are thirty-two deities which are appearances of the factors of purification of the constituents of one person. Thus, even though many deities appear in the mandala, there is really only one being.

Deity yoga is practiced for the main purpose of achieving the supreme feat of Buddhahood in order to be of full service to other sentient beings. In general, the tantric path comprises the yoga of the non-duality of the profound and the manifest. The profound is the wisdom realizing the profound emptiness of inherent existence, and the manifest is the simultaneous manifestation of that wisdom consciousness as a divine circle. The appearance factor of the consciousness manifests as a deity, mandala dwelling, and so forth, and the ascertainment factor of that same consciousness realizes the absence of inherent existence of those.

In Highest Yoga Tantra, the uncommon, special practice involves the usage of subtler levels of consciousness. In the context of this topic, the *Guhyasamāja Tantra* speaks of the three bodies of the ordinary state which are caused to appear as the three bodies of the path state, in dependence upon which the Three Buddha Bodies of the effect state are actualized. About the three bodies of the ordinary state, our ordinary death—the mind of clear light that dawns at death—is the Truth Body of the ordinary state. Similarly, except for rebirth in a Formless Realm, there is an intermediate state between death and rebirth, which is called the Complete Enjoyment Body of the ordinary state. The point of conception in the new life is called the Emanation Body of the ordinary state. In the same way, within one day, deep sleep is posited as the Truth Body of the ordinary state; dreaming is posited as the Complete Enjoyment Body of the ordinary state, and waking is posited as the Emanation Body of the ordinary state. These factors in ordinary existence are used in the path such that the corresponding factors of Buddhahood are achieved. The practice is done within deity yoga, but in addition subtler levels of mind are used, making progress over the path to Buddhahood quicker.

In deity yoga the practitioner is seeking to achieve, at best, the supreme feat of Buddhahood; at the middling level, any of the eight great feats; and at the lowest level, an activity of pacification, increase, subjugation, or ferocity—all for the sake of others' welfare. Among the deities used in such meditation there are both peaceful and wrathful forms. The reason for these many forms is this: In the scriptures of the Hearers, there is no explanation of using an afflictive emotion in the path; however, in the Bodhisattva scriptures of the Perfection Vehicle, there are explanations of using the afflictive emotions of desire in the path in the sense of using desire as an aid in accomplishing others' welfare as in the case of a Bodhisattva king's fathering many children to help the kingdom. However, in the Mantra Vehicle even hatred is explained as being used in the path. This refers to the time of implementation, not to the motivation which is just compassion. With compassion as the causal motivation, at the time of the actual practice the practitioner utilizes hatred or wrath for a specific purpose. This technique is based on the fact that when we become angry, an energetic and powerful mind is generated. When trying to achieve a fierce activity, the energy and power make a difference. Thus, it is because of the usage of hatred in the path in this way that there come to be wrathful deities.

In the hands of many peaceful and wrathful deities there are skulls and so forth. For instance, Chakrasaṃvara holds a skull with blood in it; the skull signifies bliss, and the blood symbolizes the mind realizing the emptiness of inherent existence. The reason why the skull is associated with bliss is that the basis of the bliss of the melting of the basic constituent [that is to say, the basis of sexual bliss] is said to be at the crown of the head. In a similar way, a professor of medicine at the University of Virginia explained that the ultimate source of the generation of semen is in the head. Thus, the skull filled with blood symbolizes emptiness and bliss.

In other contexts, a skull symbolizes impermanence; a corpse symbolizes selflessness. With a supramundane deity, five dry skulls symbolize the five exalted wisdoms and the five Buddha lineages. Such explanations are required for understanding a wrathful deity.

In the praises of wrathful deities it is always mentioned that they do not stir from the Truth Body or from love. If a practitioner of tantra who did not have the prerequisite of the development of strong compassion attempted such wrathful practice, it would harm rather than help. As the great Tibetan adept from Hlodrak, Namkha Gyeltsen (*lho brag nam mkha' rgyal mtshan*), said, if you practice tantra without having great love and compassion and understanding of emptiness, the repetition of fierce mantra can lead to rebirth as a bad spirit that seeks to harm beings. It is extremely important to have the prerequisites and all qualifications for the practice of tantra.

Similarly, the proper practice of the yoga of inner wind, or breath, is difficult and can be dangerous. Therefore, it is said that tantric practice must be done in secret, in hiding. It is easy to look at the pictures and statues in a museum but difficult to do the actual practice.

EIGHT VERSES FOR
TRAINING THE MIND

I AM VERY HAPPY to be visiting one of the oldest Tibetan Buddhist centers in America, and I would like to extend my warm greetings to all who have come here, particularly to the Kalmyk-Americans, who are, in comparison to us Tibetans, elder refugees. For many centuries there has been a strong relationship between the Mongolian and Tibetan peoples, by means of which Tibetan Buddhism became the Buddhism of Mongolia. Right through to the present Mongolians have mainly studied the Buddhist religion in the Tibetan language and prayed in Tibetan as well, and my own name "Dalai" was given by a Mongol chieftain. Thus the Dalai Lama has a special connection with the Mongolian people.

Under the bright sun in this fine park are gathered many who speak a variety of languages, wear different styles of dress, and are different perhaps also in religious faith. However, we are all the same in being human. We all innately have the thought "I," and we all want happiness and do not want suffering. Those who have cameras and are taking pictures, the monks sitting before me, all those standing and sitting in the audience share the thought, "May I have happiness, and may I avoid suffering." We spend our lives within such a thought appearing innately in our minds.

Further, we all equally have the right to achieve happiness and avoid suffering. From among the many different techniques for doing so, each of us has our own estimation of what the best is and leads his or her life accordingly. When we investigate to determine the nature of the happiness we seek and the suffering we wish to avoid, we find that there are many different forms of these; however, in brief, there are two types: physical pleasure and suffering, and mental pleasure and suffering.

Material progress is for the sake of achieving that happiness and relieving that suffering which depends upon the body. But it is indeed difficult to remove *all* suffering by these external means and thereby achieve complete satisfaction. Hence there comes to be a great difference between seeking happiness in dependence upon external things and seeking it in dependence upon one's own internal spiritual development. Furthermore, even if the basic suffering is the same, there is a great difference in the way we experience it and in the mental discomfort that it creates, depending upon our attitude towards it. Hence our mental attitude is very important in how we spend our lives.

There are many religions that set forth precepts and advice on how to adjust one's mental attitude, and all, without exception, are concerned with making the mind more peaceful, disciplined, moral, and ethical. In this way the essence of all religions is the same, even though in terms of philosophy there are many differences. Indeed, there would be no end to argument if we concentrated just on the philosophical differences, but this would create unnecessary work for us. Far more useful and meaningful is to try to implement in daily life the precepts for goodness that we have heard in any religion.

In a sense, a religious practitioner is actually a soldier engaged in combat. With what enemies does he or she fight? Internal ones. Ignorance, anger, attachment, and pride are the ultimate enemies;

they are not outside, but within, and must be fought with the weapons of wisdom and concentration. Wisdom is the bullet, the ammunition; concentration—the calm abiding of the mind—is the weapon for firing it. Just as when we fight an external enemy, there is injury and suffering, so also when we fight internally, there is internal pain and hardship. Thus, religion is an internal matter, and religious precepts have to do with inner development.

To approach this from another viewpoint: We are going deep into outer space based on modern science and technology developed through human thought; yet, there are many things left to be examined and thought about with respect to the nature of the mind—whether it is caused or not, and if it is caused, what its substantial cause is, what its cooperative conditions are, what its effects are, and so forth. For developing the mind, there are many precepts, and from among these, the main are love and compassion. The Buddhist doctrine has many finely developed and powerful techniques capable of advancing the mind with respect to love and compassion. A good mind, a good heart, warm feeling are most important. If you have such a good mind, you yourself will be comfortable, and your family, mate, children, parents, neighbors, and so forth will be happy as well. If you do not have such a good mind, just the opposite occurs. The reason why from nation to nation, continent to continent, people are unhappy is just this. Thus, in human society good will and kindness are the most important things. They are precious and necessary in one's life, and it is worthwhile to make effort to develop a good heart.

From every viewpoint we are all the same in wanting happiness and not wanting suffering. However, oneself is only one whereas others are infinite in number. Therefore, based on the great difference between the amount of satisfaction there is in just oneself being happy and the amount of satisfaction there is in an infinite number of people being happy, others are more important than oneself. If oneself, one person, cannot stand suffering, how can any sentient being stand it? Therefore, it is right to use oneself for others' welfare and a mistake to use others for one's own purposes.

To use whatever capacities of body, speech, and mind one has for the benefit of others, it is necessary to generate a mind of altruism wishing to remove others' suffering and to achieve others' happiness. Whether one believes in a religion or not, whether one asserts that there are former and future lifetimes or not, there is no one who does not appreciate compassion. Right from the time of birth, we are under the care and kindness of our parents. Then, later at the end of our lives when we are pressed by the suffering of aging, we are again very much reliant on the good heart and compassion of others. Since it is the case that at the beginning and end of our lives we are dependent on others' kindness, it would be only appropriate if between those two periods we cultivated a sense of kindness towards others.

No matter whom I meet and where I go, I always give advice to be altruistic, to have a good heart. I am now forty-four years old, and from the time when I began to think until now I have been cultivating this attitude of altruism. This is the essence of religion; this is the essence of the Buddhist teaching.

We should take this good heart, this altruism, as the very basis and internal structure of our practice, and should direct whatever virtuous activities we do towards its increase higher and higher. We should suffuse our minds with it thoroughly, and should also use words, writings, as means of reminding ourselves of the practice. Such words are the *Eight Stanzas for Training the Mind* written by the Kadampa Geshe Langri Thangpa (*glang ri thang pa*, 1054-1123); they are powerful even when practiced only at the level of enthusiastic interest.

1   *With a determination to accomplish*
    The highest welfare for all sentient beings
    Who surpass even a wish-granting jewel
    I will learn to hold them supremely dear.

Never mind neglecting other sentient beings, you should take them as a treasure through which temporary and final aims can be achieved and should cherish them one-pointedly. Others should be considered more dear, more important than yourself. Initially, it is in dependence upon sentient beings—others—that you generate the altruistic aspiration to highest enlightenment. In the middle, it is in relation to sentient beings that you increase this good mind higher and higher and practice the deeds of the path in order to achieve enlightenment. Finally, in the end, it is for the sake of sentient beings that you achieve Buddhahood. Since sentient beings are the aim and basis of all of this marvelous development, they are more important than even a wish-granting jewel, and should always be treated with respect, kindness, and love.

You might think, "My mind is so full of the afflictive emotions. How could I possibly do this?" However, the mind does what it is used to. What we are not used to, we find difficult, but with familiarity, previously difficult things become easy. Thus Shāntideva's *Engaging in the Bodhisattva Deeds* says, "There is nothing which, with time, you cannot get used to."

2   *Whenever I associate with others I will learn*
    To think of myself as the lowest among all
    And respectfully hold others to be supreme
    From the very depths of my heart.

If you cultivate love, compassion, and so forth for your own welfare, seeking happiness only for yourself, you are bound within a selfish viewpoint which will not lead to good results. Rather, you should have an attitude of altruism, seeking the welfare of others from the very depths of your heart.

Pride in which, cherishing yourself, you view yourself as superior and others as inferior is a major obstacle to the development of an altruistic attitude respecting and cherishing others. Therefore, it is important to rely on the antidote to pride and, no matter who you are with, to consider yourself lower than others. If you assume a humble attitude, your own good qualities will increase, whereas when you are full of pride, there is no way to be happy. You will become jealous of others, angry with them, and look down on them, due to which an unpleasant atmosphere will be created and unhappiness in society will increase.

It is on the basis of false reasons that we take pride in ourselves and feel superior to others, and, conversely, we can counter pride by reflecting on others' good qualities and our own bad qualities. Consider, for instance, this fly buzzing around me. From one viewpoint, I am a human being, a monk, and of course am much more important than this small fly. However, viewed another way, it is no surprise that this weak lowly fly who is continually overcome by obscuration is not engaged in religious practice; further, this fly is not engaged in bad actions accomplished through sophisticated techniques. I, on the other hand, as a human being with full human potential and a sophisticated mind, might misuse my capacities. Should I—a supposed practitioner, a supposed monk, a supposed human being, a supposed cultivator of the altruistic aspiration—use my capacities in a wrong way, then I am far worse than a fly. Thinking this way automatically helps.

However, maintaining a humble view of oneself in order to counter pride does not mean that you should come under the influence of those who are engaged in wrong practice. It is necessary to stop and make answer to such persons; nevertheless, although it may be necessary to give a strong reaction to someone, it should be done within an attitude of respect.

3 *In all actions I will learn to search into my mind*
  And as soon as an afflictive emotion arises
  Endangering myself and others
  Will firmly face and avert it.

If when practicing such a good altruistic attitude, you leave your afflictive emotions just as they are, they will create trouble, for anger, pride, and so forth are obstacles to the development of altruism. Thus, you should not let these go on and on but, relying on their antidotes, immediately stop them. As I said before, anger, pride, competitiveness, and so forth are our real enemies. Our battleground is not external but within.

Since there is no one who has not gotten angry at some time, we can understand on the basis of our own experience that anger does not yield happiness. Who could be happy within an attitude of anger? What doctor prescribes anger as a treatment? Who says that by getting angry you can make yourself happier? Therefore, we should not allow any opportunity for these afflictive emotions to be generated. Even though there is no one who does not value his or her own life, if we come under the influence of anger, we can even be brought to the point of wishing to commit suicide.

Having identified the various types of afflictive emotions, when even the slightest form of one begins to be generated you should not think, "This much is probably okay," because it will only become stronger and stronger, like a small fire that has started in a house. There is a Tibetan saying, "Don't make friends with 'It's-probably-okay'," for to do so is dangerous.

As soon as you start to generate an afflictive emotion you should think of the opposite type of quality, using reason to generate an opposite attitude. For instance, if you start to generate desire, reflect on ugliness or establish your mind in mindfulness of the body or mindfulness of feeling. When you get angry, cultivate love; when you generate pride, think about the twelve links of dependent-arising or the divisions of the various constituents. The basic antidote to all these faulty states is the wisdom realizing emptiness, which will be discussed in the final verse.

Most important upon generating an afflictive emotion is to rely at once on the appropriate antidote and stop it entirely before it can develop more. However, if you cannot do that, at least seek to distract your mind from the afflictive emotion—go out for a walk, or contemplate the inhalation and exhalation of the breath.

What is the fault of generating the afflictive emotions? When the mind comes under the influence of an afflictive emotion, not only do you become uncomfortable right then and there, but also this induces bad physical and verbal deeds which cause suffering in the future. For instance, anger can lead to violent words and eventually to violent physical acts in which others are hurt. These actions establish predispositions in the mind that bring about suffering in the future.

Thus it is said, "If you want to know what you were doing in the past, look at your body now; if you want to know what will happen to you in the future, look at what your mind is doing now." The Buddhist theory of actions and their effects means that our present body and general situation have been formed by our past actions and that our future happiness and suffering are in our own hands right now. Since we want happiness and do not want suffering, and since virtuous actions lead to happiness and non-

virtuous ones lead to suffering, we should give up the non-virtuous and engage in virtue. Although it is not possible in a few days
to take upon yourself the complete practice of abandoning the
non-virtuous and assuming virtue, you can gradually get used to
these and develop your practice to higher and higher levels.

4   *I will learn to cherish beings of bad nature*
      And those pressed by strong sins and sufferings
      As if I had found a precious
      Treasure very difficult to find.

When you meet with persons of bad character or those who have
some particularly strong sickness or other problems, you should
neither neglect them nor create a distance between yourself and
them, feeling them to be alien, but rather generate an especially
strong attitude of cherishing them and holding them dear. In the
past in Tibet, those who were engaged in this type of training of
the mind took on themselves the burden of serving persons who
had leprosy much as the Christian monks and so forth do nowadays. Since it is in relation to such persons that you can cultivate
the altruistic intention to become enlightened as well as patience
and the voluntary assumption of suffering, coming in contact with
them is to viewed as like finding a precious treasure.

5   *When others out of jealousy treat me badly*
      With abuse, slander, and so on,
      I will learn to take all loss
      And offer the victory to them.

Even though in the worldly way it is proper to respond strongly to someone who has unjustifiably and without reason accused you, it does not fit in with the practice of the altruistic aspiration to enlightenment. It is incorrect to respond strongly unless there is a special purpose. If someone out of jealousy or out of dislike treats you badly with abuse or even strikes you physically, rather than responding in kind, you should suffer the defeat yourself and allow the other to have the victory. Does this seem unrealistic? This type of practice is difficult indeed but must be done by those who seek one-pointedly to develop an altruistic mind.

This does not mean that in the Buddhist religion you only take the loss all the time and purposely seek out a bad state of life. The purpose of this practice is to achieve a great result though undertaking small losses. If circumstances are such that there is no great fruit to be gained through taking a small loss, then you can, without any hatred but with a motivation of compassion, respond in a strong manner.

For instance, one from among the forty-six secondary precepts of the Bodhisattva vow is to answer appropriately and halt someone who is engaged in a wrong activity. It is necessary to stop an evil action that is being done by someone else. In one of his previous births, Shākyamuni Buddha was born as the captain, the Compassionate One. On his ship were 500 traders, and among them was one who thought to kill the other 499 and take all of their goods. The captain tried many times to advise the man not to do such evil, but he held to his plan. The captain had compassion for the 499 persons who were in danger of being killed and wanted to save their lives; he also had compassion for the man who was planning to kill them and who by doing so would accumulate tremendous bad karma. Thus he decided that, having no other means to stop him, it would be better to take upon himself the karmic burden of killing one person in order to spare that person the karma of killing 499, and he killed the would-be murderer.

Because of his compassionate motivation, the captain accumulated great merit, even through a deed of killing. This is an example of the type of activity that a Bodhisattva must do in order to undertake the appropriate action to stop someone else's doing an evil deed.

6   *When one whom I have benefited with great hope*
     Unreasonably hurts me very badly,
     I will learn to view that person
     As an excellent spiritual guide.

When you have been very kind and helped another a great deal, that person should indeed reciprocate with kindness. If, instead of showing kindness, the person is ungrateful and shows a bad manner and so forth to you, it is a sad circumstance, but within the context of the practice of altruism, you should have a sense of even greater kindness toward that person. Shāntideva's *Engaging in the Bodhisattva Deeds* says that someone who acts like an enemy towards you is the best of teachers. In dependence on a spiritual teacher you can form an understanding of patience but cannot gain an opportunity to practice patience; the actual practice of implementing patience comes when you encounter an enemy.

In order to develop true and unbiased love and compassion, you must develop patience, and this requires practice. Therefore, one training in altruism should think of an enemy as the best of spiritual teachers and, considering that person in this sense to be kind, view him or her with respect.

It is not necessary that someone or something have a good motivation towards you for you to have a sense of respect and cherishing. For instance, the doctrines that we are seeking to achieve, the true cessations of suffering and so forth, do not have any motivation at all, and yet we cherish, value, and respect them highly. Thus, the presence or absence of motivation makes no difference in terms of whether something can be helpful for increasing good qualities and accumulating merit.

Still, motivation—a wish to harm—is the basis for determining whether someone is an enemy or not. A doctor, for instance, may cause us pain performing an operation, but since the doctor has done it from a motivation to help we do not consider him or her an enemy. It is only in relation to those wishing us harm—enemies—that we can truly cultivate patience, and thus an enemy is absolutely necessary; it cannot be cultivated in relation to your lama.

There is a Tibetan story of a fellow who, while circumambulating a temple, saw someone sitting in meditative posture. He asked the meditator what he was doing, and the meditator answered, "I am cultivating patience." Then that person said something harsh to the meditator and the meditator at once answered back angrily. This response came because although he had been cultivating patience, he had not encountered anyone who was harming him or speaking badly to him; he had had no chance to *practice* patience. Thus, the best of all situations for the practice of patience is an enemy, and for this reason someone engaged in the Bodhisattva practices should treat an enemy with tremendous respect.

Without tolerance, without patience, you cannot develop true compassion. In the ordinary way, compassion is usually mixed with attachment, and because of that it is difficult to feel compassion for your enemies. You have to work to develop true love and compassion which extend even to enemies—those whose motivation is to harm you—and for this you need the experience of dealing with enemies. The most difficult period in one's life is the best chance to gain real experience and inner strength. If your life goes very easily, you become soft; when passing through the most tragic circumstances you can develop inner strength, the courage to face them, without emotional feeling. Who teaches this? Not your friend, not your guru, but your enemy.

7   *In short, I will learn to offer to everyone without exception*
          All help and happiness directly and indirectly
          And respectfully take upon myself
          All harm and suffering of my mothers.

This stanza sets forth the practice of giving and taking—out of love giving your happiness and causes of happiness to others and out of compassion taking from others their suffering and the causes that would make them suffer. These are the two main attitudes of a Bodhisattva: compassion caring about others' suffering and love wishing for others to have happiness. When, training in these two, you come upon people who are manifestly undergoing suffering, you should practice giving and taking, thinking:

> This person is suffering very badly and, though wanting to gain happiness and alleviate suffering, does not know how to give up non-virtues and adopt virtuous practices; hence he/she is bereft of happiness. I will take this person's suffering and give this person all of my happiness.

Although there may be exceptional persons who actually can physically do this, it is very rare; most of us can only imagine it. However, mentally doing this practice of removing suffering from others and taking it upon yourself is helpful internally and has the effect of increasing the determination to do so in actuality. This practice is done in conjunction with the inhalation and exhalation of the breath—inhaling others' pain and exhaling your happiness to them.

8 *I will learn to keep all these practices*
Undefiled by the stains of the eight worldly conceptions
And by understanding all phenomena as like illusions
Be released from the bondage of attachment.

In terms of method, these practices should be done one-pointedly within altruistically seeking the benefit of others; you should not come under the influence of the eight worldly styles of behavior—like and dislike, gaining and losing, praise and blame, fame and disgrace. If these practices are done with a motivation to inflate yourself, to cause others to think that you are a religious person, to gain renown, and so forth, then the practice is not pure but has become defiled by worldly concerns. Instead, virtue should be totally for the sake of others.

The latter part of the stanza refers to the factor of wisdom: You should engage in this practice from the viewpoint of knowing that compassion itself, the practitioner of compassion, and the objects of compassion are like a magician's illusions in that they appear to exist inherently but do not. In order to understand these three factors as like illusions, it is necessary to know that even though these factors appear to be inherently existent, they are empty of such inherent existence.

For instance, if persons working at the altruistic intention to become enlightened were to view themselves as existing in their own right, or were to view the persons for whose sake enlightenment is being sought as inherently existent, or were to view enlightenment itself as inherently existent, this viewing of inherent existence would in fact prevent that meditator from achieving enlightenment. Instead, it is necessary to view yourself—the cultivator of the altruistic intention—the enlightenment you are seeking, and all other sentient beings—those for whom you are seeking enlightenment—as not inherently existent, but rather as like illusions, existing one way but appearing in another. By means of viewing these as like illusions their inherent existence is refuted.

This refutation of inherent existence is not a case of removing something that formerly existed. Rather, you are identifying that something that never did exist does not exist. Due to our own ignorance, phenomena appear to exist inherently even though they do not; due to this appearance of inherent existence, we conceive that things exist the way they appear; due to that, we are drawn into afflictive emotions and thereby are ruined. For instance, you look at me and think, "There is the Dalai Lama," and suddenly, without any fabrication, it seems to your mind that there is a Dalai Lama separate from his body and independent even of his mind. Or, consider yourself. If your name is David, for instance, we say, "David's body, David's mind," and it seems to you that there is a David who owns his mind and body and a mind and body that this David owns, does it not? We say that the Dalai Lama is a monk, a human, a Tibetan. Does it not seem that you are saying this not with respect to his body or his mind, but that there is something independent?

Persons do exist, but they do so only nominally, through designation. Yet, when they appear to our minds, they appear not as existing through the force of being posited by names and terminology but as if they exist in their own right, able to set themselves up, self-instituting. Although it is a fact that phenomena do not exist in and of themselves but depend on something else for their very existence, they appear to us to be independent.

If things did in fact exist the way they appear—if things did exist so concretely—then when one looked into and investigated them, this inherent existence should become even clearer, more obvious. However, when you seek for the object designated, you cannot find it under analysis. For instance, conventionally there is an "I" undergoing pleasure and pain, accumulating karma, and so forth, but when we analytically search for this "I" we cannot find it. No matter what the phenomenon is, internal or external, whether it be one's own body or any other type of phenomenon, when we search to discover what this phenomenon that is designated is, we cannot find anything that is it.

This which gives rise to the appearance of "I" is mind and body, but when you divide this into mind and body and look for the "I," you cannot find it. Also the whole, the body, is designated in dependence upon the collection of the parts of the body; if you divide this into its parts and look for the body, you cannot find it either.

Even the most subtle particles in the body have sides and hence parts. Were there something partless, it might be independent, but there is nothing that is partless. Rather, everything exists in dependence on its parts, is only designated in dependence on its parts—its basis of designation—through the force of conceptuality; there is nothing analytically findable. There is no whole which is separate from its parts.

However, these things appear to us as if they do exist objectively and in their own right, and thus there is a difference between the way things appear to our minds and the way they actually exist, or the way we see them to exist when we analyze. If they did exist in accordance with how they appear to be established in their own right, this mode of existence should become clearer and clearer as we investigate. Yet, we can come to a decision through our own experience that when we search for these things, analytically we cannot find them. Thus they are said to be like illusions.

Since phenomena appear to us in a way that is different from what we discover when analyzing, this proves that their concrete appearance is due to a fault of our minds. After you understand that these phenomena appearing to exist in their own right are empty of existing in the way that they appear, you have realization of phenomena as like illusions in that there is a composite of knowing the appearance of phenomena and understanding that they are empty of existing in the way they appear.

What is the benefit of understanding this? Our afflictive emotions of desire, hatred, and so forth arise because we superimpose upon phenomena a goodness and badness beyond that which they actually have. For instance, when we get angry or desirous, we have during that time a strong sense of the goodness or badness of that object, but later when these emotions calm down and we look at those same objects, we ourselves will even find our earlier perception laughable. The benefit or assistance of wisdom is that it prevents us from superimposing on objects a goodness or badness beyond what is actually there, whereby we are able to stop desire and hatred.

Thus, the two parts of this unified practice are method and wisdom—method being the cultivation of the altruistic attitudes of love and compassion and wisdom being the view understanding the absence of inherent existence of all phenomena. These two must be in union.

I recite these verses every day and, when I meet with difficult circumstances, reflect on their meaning. It helps me. Thinking that they might help others as well, I have explained them here. If this helps your mind, practice it. If it does not help, there is no debate; just leave it. The dharma, or doctrine, is not for the sake of controversy. These teachings were spoken by the great masters in order to help, not for people to quarrel with each other. Were I as a Buddhist to quarrel with a person of some other religion, then, I think, if Buddha were here today, he would scold me. The doctrine is to be brought into our own mental continuum for the sake of taming it.

In conclusion, my request, my appeal, is that you try as much as you can to develop compassion, love, and respect for others, to share others' suffering, to have more concern for others' welfare, and to become less selfish. Whether you believe in God or not, in Buddha or not, does not matter. The important thing is to have a good heart, a warm heart, in daily life. This is the principle of life.

Oṃ Maṇi Padme Hūṃ

IT IS BENEFICIAL to recite the mantra *oṃ maṇi padme hūṃ,* but while you are doing it, you should be thinking on its meaning, for the meaning of the six syllables is great and vast. The first, *oṃ,* is composed of three letters, *a, u,* and *m.* These symbolize the practitioner's impure body, speech, and mind; they also symbolize the pure exalted body, speech, and mind of a Buddha.

Can impure body, speech, and mind be transformed into the pure, or are they entirely separate? All Buddhas are cases of beings who were like ourselves and then in dependence on the path became enlightened; Buddhism does not assert that there is anyone who from the beginning is free from faults and possesses all good qualities. The development of pure body, speech, and mind comes from gradually leaving impure states and their being transformed into the pure.

How is this done? The path is indicated by the next four syllables. *Maṇi,* meaning jewel, symbolizes the factors of method—the altruistic intention to become enlightened, compassion, and love. Just as a jewel is capable of removing poverty, so the altruistic mind of enlightenment is capable of removing the poverty, or difficulties, of cyclic existence and of solitary peace. Similarly, just as a jewel fulfills the wishes of sentient beings, so the altruistic intention to become enlightened fulfills the wishes of sentient beings.

The two syllables, *padme,* meaning lotus, symbolize wisdom. Just as a lotus grows forth from mud but is not sullied by the faults of mud, so wisdom is capable of putting you in a situation of non-contradiction, whereas there would be contradiction if you did not have wisdom. There is wisdom realizing impermanence, wisdom realizing that persons are empty of being self-sufficient or substantially existent, wisdom realizing the emptiness of duality— that is to say, the lack of difference of entity between subject and object—and wisdom realizing the emptiness of inherent existence. Though there are many different types of wisdom, the main of all these is the wisdom realizing emptiness.

Purity must be achieved by an indivisible unity of method and wisdom, symbolized by the final syllable *hūṃ,* which indicates indivisibility. According to the sūtra system, this indivisibility of method and wisdom refers to wisdom affected by method and method affected by wisdom. In the mantra, or tantric, vehicle, it refers to one consciousness in which there is the full form of both wisdom and method as one undifferentiable entity. In terms of the seed syllables of the five Conqueror Buddhas, *hūṃ* is the seed syllable of Akṣhobhya—the immovable, the unfluctuating, that which cannot be disturbed by anything.

Thus the six syllables, *oṃ maṇi padme hūṃ,* mean that in dependence on the practice of a path that is an indivisible union of method and wisdom, you can transform your impure body, speech, and mind into the pure exalted body, speech, and mind of a Buddha. It is said that you should not seek for Buddhahood outside of yourself; the substances for the achievement of Buddhahood are within. As Maitreya says in his *Sublime Continuum of the Great Vehicle* (*uttaratantra, rgyud bla ma*), all beings naturally have the Buddha nature in their own continuum. We have within us the seed of purity, the matrix-of-One-Gone-Thus, that is to be transformed and fully developed into Buddhahood.

THE PATH
TO ENLIGHTENMENT

TORONTO, CANADA, AND TIBETAN BUDDHIST
LEARNING CENTER, WASHINGTON, NEW JERSEY

I AM VERY HAPPY to have the opportunity to give a lecture here in Toronto, Canada, to this assembly of Buddhists and persons interested in Buddhism. I would like to thank the Zen masters of this temple and the many Tibetans who have helped with the preparations. Today I will talk about the stages of the path to enlightenment, using Tsongkhapa's *Three Principal Aspects of the Path to Supreme Enlightenment* as a basis.

In order to be freed from cyclic existence, it is necessary to generate the intention to leave cyclic existence; this intention is the first of the three principal aspects of the path to enlightenment. It is also necessary to have the correct view of emptiness. In addition, if one wishes to achieve the highest liberation, the state of omniscience of the Great Vehicle, it is necessary to cultivate an altruistic intention to become enlightened, called the mind of enlightenment. These three—the determination to be freed from cyclic existence, the correct view of emptiness, and the altruistic mind of enlightenment—are the three principal aspects of the path.

Prior to giving a lecture, it is customary first to clear away obstacles. In Japan and Tibet, this is usually done by reciting the *Heart*

Sūtra, which is concerned with the teachings on the emptiness of inherent existence; then, in order to tame harmful beings and remove obstacles, it is helpful to recite the mantra of a fierce manifestation in female form of the perfection of wisdom. Usually, when we recite mantra, we count the mantras on a rosary, moving the beads inward as a symbol of the entry of the blessings from the recitation; however, when the purpose of the recitation is to remove obstacles, the beads are turned in the opposite direction, outward, symbolizing the removal of those obstacles.

Next, we perform the offering of mandala. The meaning of this derives from the actions of the Buddha, who, in former lifetimes while training on the path, underwent a great many hardships without concern for his body, family, or resources, in order to hear and practice the teachings. As a symbol of this dedication and unselfishness, we make, prior to listening to Buddha's teachings, a mental offering of our body, resources, and roots of virtue. The entire world system which has been formed by our collective karma is offered, visualized in a glorified aspect, full of marvels and wonders.

Whether lecturing on the doctrine or listening to it, our attitude must be conjoined with a mind of refuge and a mind of altruism that is seeking to help others. To achieve this, a verse of refuge and mind generation is recited three times in conjunction with mental reflection and meditation:

> Until enlightenment I go for refuge to the Buddha,
> The doctrine, and the supreme of communities.
> Through the merit of listening to the doctrine
> May I achieve Buddhahood in order to help transmigrating
> beings.

In that good or bad effects arise in dependence upon good or bad motivation, cultivation of an altruistic motivation is crucial. Thus, as the stanza is recited, its meaning should be cultivated in meditation.

Finally, at the beginning of a lecture on the doctrine there is a custom of repeating a stanza of praise to Buddha within being mindful of his kindness. This verse is taken from Nāgārjuna's *Treatise on the Middle* (*madhayamakaśāstra, dbu ma'i bstan bcos*),[3] and the custom of reciting it was initiated by one of my teachers, Kunu Lama Tenzin Gyeltsen (*bstan 'dzin rgyal mtshan*):

> I pay homage to Gautama
> Who, motivated by compassion,
> Taught the excellent doctrine
> In order to eliminate all [wrong] views.

Generally speaking, we have come together here because we share an interest in Buddhist doctrine; we hope by our efforts to attain greater peace in our lives and to eliminate suffering as much as possible. Since we have bodies, we need food, clothing, shelter, and so forth, but these alone are not sufficient, for satisfying just these needs cannot fulfill the wishes of human beings. No matter how good our physical surroundings are, if there is no happiness in our minds, then unrest, depression, and so forth make it impossible for us to be at ease. We need to be able to seek out and achieve mental happiness, and knowing how to do this will enable us to overpower physical sufferings as well. Therefore, it is essential to combine effort for gaining external improvement with that focused on internal concerns.

Western civilization has made and continues to make great progress in material development, but if techniques can also be created for achieving internal happiness, modern society will become far more advanced. Without such internal growth, we become enslaved to external things, and even though called humans, we become like parts of a machine. Thus our discussion today will be concerned with how to achieve mental happiness and advancement.

Throughout history, many teachers have appeared, drawing on their own experience, to advise and guide others toward more fruitful ways of living. From among these many systems of advice, I will be speaking about that offered to humanity by the kind teacher, Shākyamuni Buddha. Within his teachings, levels of practice were delineated in accordance with the capacities of his followers. These fall into two major divisions, or vehicles: the Hearer Vehicle and the Great Vehicle. Within the Great Vehicle, Buddha set forth a sūtra system and a mantra system, distinguished by differing elements in the general corpus of the path for achieving the Buddha Bodies.

In addition, Buddha further defined four separate schools of tenets: Great Exposition School (*vaibhāṣika, bye brag smra ba*), Sūtra School (*sautrāntika, mdo sde pa*), Mind-Only School (*cittamātra, sems tsam pa*), and Middle Way School (*mādhyamika, dbu ma pa*). These teachings of the two vehicles and of the four schools of tenets, as well as the sūtra and tantra systems, are contained in approximately one hundred volumes of texts translated mainly from Sanskrit into Tibetan. Nearly two hundred volumes of commentary on these scriptures were written by Indian scholars and subsequently translated into Tibetan as well.

The scriptures are divided into four main groups: texts on discipline, which are mainly concerned with practices common to the Hearer Vehicle, a section on the perfection of wisdom, a collection of various sūtras, and a section on tantra. According to the *Vajrapañjara Tantra,* an explanatory tantra, there are, within the tantra system, four sets of tantras: Action, Performance, Yoga, and Highest Yoga Tantra.[4]

The systems of sūtra, tantra, the Hearer Vehicle, and the Great

Vehicle were spread throughout Tibet. Over time, based on various methods of transmission from particular teachers and distinctive usage of certain philosophical terms, there came to be slight differences in their interpretation and use. Many different schools evolved in Tibet, and these, in brief, can be condensed into four major schools which carry on the lineage of Buddha's teaching to the present time: Nyingma, Sakya, Kagyu, and Geluk. Despite their superficial differences, these schools all come down to the same basic thought.

Today's text, the *Three Principal Aspects of the Path,* is a rendition of the many stages of the path into three principal paths, as set forth by Tsongkhapa (1357-1419). Although this text is concerned with the entire body of scripture, its main source is the Perfection of Wisdom Sūtras.

In what way do these teachings derive from the Perfection of Wisdom Sūtras? Contained within those sūtras is the explicit teaching of emptiness and the hidden teaching of the stages of the path. From among the three principal aspects of the path, that aspect concerned with the correct view of reality stems from the explicit teachings of emptiness. Presentations of the correct view in the Great Vehicle are done in accordance with the Mind-Only and Middle Way Schools. Tsongkhapa's text is based solely on the Middle Way system and, within the subdivisions of that school, is explicitly concerned with the Consequence School (*prāsaṅgika, thal 'gyur pa*) rather than the Autonomy School (*svātantrika, rang rgyud pa*). It presents just the view of the Consequence School on emptiness. The remaining aspects of the path—the determination to become free from cyclic existence and the altruistic mind of enlightenment—derive from the hidden teachings in the Perfection of Wisdom Sūtras on the paths and stages for achieving clear realization.

Two types of commentary on the Perfection of Wisdom Sūtras

have developed: the system of explanation transmitted from Mañjushrī through Nāgārjuna that has to do with the explicit teachings on emptiness and that transmitted from Maitreya through Asaṅga on the hidden teachings on the stages of the path. Maitreya's *Ornament for Clear Realization* (*abhisamayālaṃkāra, mngon rtogs rgyan*) is the root text setting forth the hidden teaching of the stages on the path. It contains eight chapters: the first three set out the three exalted knowledges; the next four describe the practices of the four trainings; and the eighth chapter describes the effect truth body. A comparison of Maitreya's text with the Perfection of Wisdom Sūtras shows that those sūtras are indeed the source for the teaching in the *Ornament for Clear Realization* of the hidden teachings on the stages of the path.

The motivation for listening to this teaching on the three principal aspects of the path should not be to gain personal benefit but rather to bring about health and happiness for all sentient beings throughout space since each and every one of them wants happiness and does not want suffering.

Now, to begin the text itself: At the beginning of composing a text it is customary for the author to pay homage to a high object, and this can be any of a number of objects of reverence. Here, Tsongkhapa pays homage to the "foremost holy lamas," for it is in dependence upon a qualified lama that the three principal aspects of the path are realized.

The high title "lama" alone does not qualify someone as a lama; the good qualities associated with the title must also be present. The three words—foremost (*rje*), holy (*btsun*), and lama (*bla ma*)—set forth the three qualities of a lama. "Foremost" describes a person who has diminished emphasis on this lifetime and is primarily concerned with future lifetimes and deeper topics. Such a person has a longer perspective than the shortsighted one of those who mainly look to the affairs of this life and thus, in relation to common beings whose emphasis is mainly on this life, is the foremost, or a leader. "Holy" refers to one who, as a result of developing renunciation for all forms of cyclic existence, is not attached to any of its marvels and is seeking liberation. A holy person has turned his or her mind away from attachment outside to the better things of cyclic existence and focused it within. In the word "lama," "la" means high, and "ma" is a negative, which indicates that there is none higher; this is a person who has turned away from self-cherishing to cherishing others, has turned away from the lower concern for personal benefit in order to achieve the higher purpose of attaining benefit for others.

In applying these three words to the teachings in Tsongkhapa's *Great Exposition of the Stages of the Path (lam rim chen mo)*,[5] the word "foremost" is connected with the paths of a being of small capacity, the word "holy" is connected with the paths of a being of middling capacity, and the word "lama" is connected with the paths of a being of great capacity. One who possesses all three levels is a "foremost holy lama." An earlier lama in Tibet made the connection between these three words here and the three levels of the path as the qualifications of a lama, but it is by no means necessary to use these three words strictly in this manner on all occasions. It is important to distinguish the context of terms used in Buddhist texts; to apply a single meaning of a term in all different contexts can lead to confusion in understanding the meaning of a text.

Tsongkhapa pays homage to the foremost holy lamas who possess these qualifications in order to express his respect for them. A respectful attitude is maintained toward one's lamas for the sake of generating these three realizations within our own mental continuums. The meaning of the Tibetan word for homage, when broken down into its component syllables, is to want an unchangeable or indivertible state. In paying homage, Tsongkhapa is expressing a wish for unchangeable, indivertible understanding of these three topics.

Tsongkhapa met and studied with many lamas of the Nyingma, Sakya, and Kagyu orders and, in particular, met personally with Mañjushrī and in dependence upon his kindness generated the non-erroneous view realizing the profound emptiness. In addition, it was the quintessential instruction of Mañjushrī to condense all the teachings of the path into these three principal aspects. Thus, it is to these holy lamas that Tsongkhapa pays homage at the beginning of the text:[6]

> Homage to the foremost holy lamas.

The promise to compose the text is contained in the first stanza:

> I will explain as well as I can
> The essential meaning of all the Conqueror's scriptures,
> The path praised by the excellent Conqueror Children,
> The port for the fortunate wishing liberation.

It is suitable to explain the last three lines of this stanza as referring to one thing, in which case they would read: "the essential meaning of all the Conqueror's scriptures, which is the path praised by the excellent Conqueror Children and is the port for the fortunate wishing liberation." However, these lines can also be taken as referring individually to the three principal aspects of the path. The first, "the essential meaning of all the Conqueror's scriptures," represents the determination to be freed from cyclic existence. "The path praised by the excellent Conqueror Children" refers to the altruistic intention to become enlightened, and "the port for the fortunate wishing liberation" indicates the correct view of emptiness.

How does the "the essential meaning of all the Conqueror's scriptures" refer to the determination to be freed from cyclic existence? As Tsongkhapa says in his *Praise of Dependent-Arising* (*rten 'brel stod pa*):[7]

All of your various teachings
Are solely based on dependent-arising
And are for sake of passing from sorrow.
You have nothing that does not tend toward peace.

All of Buddha's teachings are for the purpose of trainees' attaining freedom from cyclic existence; Buddha taught nothing that is not for the sake of peace. Since the determination to be freed from cyclic existence forms the root of the path that is the unmistaken means of achieving liberation, it is the essential meaning of all the Conqueror's scriptures.

In the next line, "the path praised by the excellent Conqueror Children," the term "Conqueror Children" (*jinaputra, rgyal sras*) refers to Bodhisattvas, beings who are born from the speech of the Conqueror Buddha. The path praised by them refers to the altruistic intention to become enlightened. Through generating the altruistic mind of enlightenment, one becomes a Bodhisattva, and by means of it one is able to help others.

"The port for the fortunate wishing liberation" refers to the correct view of emptiness. For it is through this view that we can be freed from cyclic existence. As Āryadeva's *Four Hundred* (*catuḥśataka, bzhi brgya pa*) says,[8] "the door of peace of which there is no second." Liberation is achieved only after the afflictive emotions and so forth are removed, and this must be accomplished by means of generating in our continuum their actual antidote, the correct view realizing the emptiness of inherent existence, and familiarizing with it again and again. Lacking the correct view of emptiness, we can never be liberated from cyclic existence, regardless of other good qualities we may possess.

In the first verse, Tsongkhapa says that he will explain these three topics as well as he can. The meaning of this is either that he is assuming a humble attitude prior to composing the text or that he will do his best to explain these three topics in brief terms. In fact, at the time Tsongkhapa wrote the *Three Principal Aspects of the Path,* he had already, much earlier in his life, generated the determination to become free from cyclic existence and the altruistic intention to become enlightened as well as the view of emptiness according to its uncommon explanation in the Consequence School. He had also arrived at the completion stage of Highest Yoga Tantra, having attained either the first level, verbal isolation, or the second level, mental isolation, from among the five levels of the completion stage in Highest Yoga Tantra according to the *Guhyasamāja Tantra.*[9]

In the next stanza Tsongkhapa makes an exhortation to those who are fit vessels for the doctrine to listen to this teaching:

Whoever are not attached to the pleasures of mundane existence,
Whoever strive in order to make leisure and fortune worthwhile,
Whoever are inclined to the path pleasing the Conqueror Buddha,
Those fortunate ones should listen with a clear mind.

The three topics mentioned in this stanza can also be applied to the three principal aspects of the path. Non-attachment to the pleasures of mundane existence refers to having the determination to be freed from cyclic existence. Making leisure and fortune worthwhile suggests that if the altruistic intention to become enlightened is generated, then the leisure and fortune which we humans have is being used in a meaningful and worthwhile manner. Being inclined to the path that pleases the Conqueror Buddha refers to an interested and faithful person's generating the correct view of emptiness in meditation; making use of an unmistaken path proceeding to liberation, one thereby fulfills Buddha's purpose in teaching the path. A person who is an appropriate listener to this text should possess a profound interest from the depths of the heart in the three principal aspects of the path to enlightenment, and thus Tsongkhapa states, "Those fortunate ones should listen."

Tsongkhapa speaks of the purpose for generating the determination to become free from cyclic existence:

> *Without a complete thought definitely to leave cyclic existence*
> *There is no way to stop seeking pleasurable effects in the ocean of*
> *   existence.*
> *Also, craving cyclic existence thoroughly binds the embodied.*
> *Therefore, in the beginning determination to leave cyclic existence*
> *   should be sought.*

Without this complete determination, there is no way to stop seeking pleasurable experience in the ocean of existence, and it is this craving for cyclic existence that thoroughly binds beings, illustrated here by those who have bodies. Therefore, in setting out on the path to enlightenment, it is important to develop a strong determination definitely to get out of cyclic existence. As Āryadeva says:[10]

> How could whoever is not discouraged about this
> Be intent on pacification?

A person who cannot generate a sense of discouragement when looking at the artifacts of cyclic existence is incapable of generating the attitude of seeking liberation, peace.

To generate such a thought it is first necessary to understand the advantages of liberation and the faults of cyclic existence. Dhar-makīrti describes cyclic existence as the burden of mental and physical aggregates assumed under the influence of contaminated actions and afflictions.[11] Hence, cyclic existence is not a place or an area but is to be identified within ourselves. Because our aggregates—our minds and bodies—are a consequence of former contaminated actions and afflictive emotions, they are not under our own control. This means that even though we want happiness and wish to avoid suffering, we are beset by many unwanted sufferings and lack the happiness we want because our minds and bodies are controlled by former actions and afflictions. Once we have acquired such contaminated aggregates, they serve as the basis of the suffering we experience in the present and they also induce suffering in the future.

We very much value what we perceive to be our own; we say "my body" or "my mental and physical aggregates," cherishing them greatly. Yet, that which we cherish has actually a nature of suffering. Though we do not want birth, aging, sickness, or death, these unwanted sufferings arise in dependence upon the contaminated mental and physical aggregates we so much value. In order to alleviate this suffering we must question whether there is a technique for removing the contaminated mental and physical aggregates. Are these aggregates produced in dependence on causes, or are they produced causelessly? If they did not depend on causes, they could not change, but we know that they do change, and this indicates their dependence on causes; the mental and physical aggregates each have their respective substantial causes and co-operative conditions. Our minds having come under the influence of afflictive emotions, we engage in actions that establish in the mind predispositions impelling future cyclic existences. This is the contaminated process that forms our mental and physical aggregates into having a nature of suffering.

We possess mental and physical aggregates now, and we will still possess them when we attain Buddhahood, but the causation of the mental and physical aggregates of cyclic existence is rooted in the contaminated process that results from an uncontrolled mind and the actions that come from it. Therefore, it is possible to separate the mental and physical aggregates from the process of contaminated causation and thus from having a nature of suffering and yet their continuum remains in a pure form.

To remove the aggregates that are under the influence of contaminated actions and afflictions and thereby have a nature of suffering, it is necessary to stop the new accumulation of contaminated actions (*karma, las*) as well as to stop nourishing contaminated karmas which were previously accumulated. For this, it is necessary to remove the afflictive emotions.

There are many different types of afflictive emotions. As Vasubandhu's *Treasury of Manifest Knowledge* says,[12] "The roots of cyclic existence are the six subtle increasers [of contamination]." That text speaks of five views and five non-views; the five views are then condensed into one and, combined with the five non-view afflictions, comprise the six basic root afflictions: desire, anger, pride, doubt, afflictive view, and obscuration. The root of all these afflictions is ignorance.

Ignorance can be identified in many different ways. From the viewpoint of the highest system, the Middle Way Consequence School, it is described as the conception of objects as having inherent existence, whereas in fact they do not. Through the force of such ignorance, the other afflictive emotions are then generated. When we analyze whether this ignorance is intrinsic to the nature of the mind itself, we will find that, as Dharmakīrti says,[13] "The nature of the mind is clear light; the defilements are adventitious." Once the defilements do not subsist in the nature of the mind, it is possible to remove them through generating an antidote to them.

We are thoroughly habituated to the mistaken conception that objects truly exist, but this conception has no valid foundation. The opposite of it is the realization that phenomena do not inherently exist, and although we are not accustomed to this view, there are reasons that establish the absence of inherent existence of phenomena; hence it has valid foundation, and through becoming familiar with the reasons establishing it, it is possible to generate the wisdom that is the opposite of ignorance.

Whereas ignorance and the wisdom realizing the absence of inherent existence both have the same object of observation—any phenomenon—their mode of apprehension of that object is exactly opposite. Wisdom has a valid foundation and is well reasoned, whereas ignorance has no valid foundation and is mistaken with respect to what it is conceiving. Thus, we can understand from our own experience that by increasing the strength of wisdom, ignorance will weaken. Qualities of mind are stable in that as long as their functioning has not deteriorated, it is not necessary to rely on new exertion for them to continue to exist. Therefore, it can be established that the wisdom that realizes selflessness can be generated and, as one familiarizes with it more and more, can eventually be increased limitlessly. When it is produced to its full extent, wisdom will cause ignorance—the mind that apprehends the opposite, inherent existence—gradually to decrease and finally to disappear entirely.

Afflictions and defilements are thus extinguished in the sphere of reality. Upon the extinction of the adventitious defilements through the power of their antidote, this purified sphere of reality is called liberation. The fact that the mind has a nature of luminosity and knowing is the basis for establishing that liberation can be achieved.

From another point of view, liberation is attained by knowing the final nature of the mind itself; it is not received from an outside source; it is not bestowed on us by someone else. By achieving liberation, the afflictive emotions are all removed, and due to this, regardless of the nature of the external conditions we encounter, we will no longer generate any afflictive emotions nor accumulate any new karma. The process of liberation depends upon the removal of the afflictive emotions, the chief of which is ignorance, and this in turn depends upon the generation of its antidote, wisdom. Since wisdom depends upon the determination to be freed from cyclic existence, without such determination liberation is impossible. Therefore, initially it is important to develop the intention to leave cyclic existence. If you see the disadvantages of cyclic existence, you will lose attraction to it, generating an aspiration toward liberation from it. Through developing that wish, you will make effort at the techniques for getting out of cyclic existence.

The next stanza describes how to train in this attitude:

Leisure and fortune are difficult to find
And life has no duration,
Through familiarity with this,
Emphasis on the appearances of this life is reversed.

Through familiarity with the fact that "leisure and fortune are difficult to find and life has no duration," our usual emphasis on the appearances of this life is reversed. In this text, the determination to leave cyclic existence is generated through reflection in two stages: first, to remove the emphasis on appearances in this life and then to remove emphasis on appearances in future lifetimes. In Tsongkhapa's *Great Exposition of the Stages of the Path,* practices for beings of small and middling capacity as well as the temporary fruits to be gained from these practices are described separately. Here in the *Three Principal Aspects,* however, these practices are merged within the one thought of developing the intention to leave cyclic existence.

There is no sense in being attached to this lifetime. No matter how long we live, which can be at most around one hundred years, eventually we must die, losing this valuable human life; further, it is indefinite when that will be—it could be any time. This life will disintegrate, and no matter how much prosperity we have, it will not help. No amount of wealth can buy an extension on life, and no matter how much money we have accumulated and have in the bank, even if we are millionaires, on the day of our death none of it can help; we have to leave it all. In this respect, the death of a millionaire and the death of a wild animal are alike. Though resources are necessary to life, they are certainly not a final object of attainment. Also, in spite of material wealth and progress, many types of suffering persist just by the fact that we have a human life, bringing unhappiness in many different ways, back to back.

Is it the very nature of human life that it be miserable? Is it unalterably so? Under the present circumstances, influenced by the process of conditioning we now experience, the very nature of life is indeed miserable. However, by means of the reasoning just set forth that establishes the possibility of attaining liberation, we can see that the causes producing misery can be overcome through separating the mind from the afflictive emotions. Thus, it is clear that misery is not necessarily inherent to human existence. If we are able to make appropriate use of human thought, we can achieve something that is valuable, whereas if we are concerned only with the affairs of this lifetime, we will waste this opportunity to use the powerful human brain we have already attained. Like investing a fortune to obtain something insignificant, the use of the human brain to achieve something of little import is very sad. Realizing the weakness of such action, we need to generate the view that an emphasis solely on the affairs of this lifetime is silly, foolish. By cultivating this attitude, the determination to leave cyclic existence, such emphasis will gradually weaken.

In renouncing this life, we do not simply ignore essential needs, such as hunger, but strive to reduce our attachment to affairs limited to this lifetime. Moreover, not just this lifetime but all of the marvelous prosperity and boundless resources of cyclic existence also have a nature of suffering, for ultimately they will deteriorate. Though one might attain a good lifetime in the future, there will be another after it, and another and another with no certainty that they will all be good. Thus, it is necessary not only to reduce our emphasis on the appearances of this lifetime but to remove attachment to future lives as well. We need to generate the thought that any lifetime under the influence of contaminated actions and afflictions is without essence, pithless.

Tsongkhapa says:

> *If you think again and again*
> *About deeds and their inevitable effects*
> *And the sufferings of cyclic existence,*
> *The emphasis on the appearances*
> *Of future lives will be reversed.*

Countless rebirths lie ahead, both good and bad. The effects of karma (actions) are inevitable, and in previous lifetimes we have accumulated negative karmas that will inevitably have their fruition in this or future lives. Just as someone witnessed by police in a criminal act will eventually be caught and punished, so we too must inevitably face the consequences of faulty actions we have committed in the past even if we are not yet in prison. Once we have accumulated predispositions for suffering from non-virtuous actions in the past, there is no way to be at ease; those actions are irreversible; we must eventually undergo their effects.

If we are unable to remove the negative karma accumulated from past faulty actions, which is already present in seed form in our own minds, there is not much hope of gaining rebirths that are wholly good or in escaping the inevitable suffering of cyclic existence. Not only that, but also when we examine the better side of cyclic existence, we find that it does not pass beyond having a nature of suffering, eventually deteriorating. Life is afflicted with three types of suffering: the suffering of pain itself, the suffering of change, and the pervasive suffering of conditioning.

By analyzing the inevitable consequences of previous faulty actions as well as the nature of suffering of even the marvels of cyclic existence we can lessen attachment to this and future lifetimes, developing the sense that liberation must be achieved. By combining these two thoughts —to overcome emphasis on the appearances of this life as well as emphasis on the marvels of cyclic existence in general—the determination to be freed from cyclic existence is generated.

What draws us into suffering—an untamed mind—is not external but within our own mental continuums. For it is through the appearance of afflictive emotions in our minds that we are drawn into various faulty actions. From the naturally pure sphere of the true nature of the mind these conceptions dawn, and through their force we engage in faulty actions leading to suffering. We need, with great awareness and care, to cause these conceptions to be extinguished back into the sphere of the nature of the mind, like clouds that gather in the sky and then dissolve back into sphere of the sky. Thereby the faulty actions that arise from them will also cease. As Milarepa (*mi la ras pa*) says, "whether arising, arising within space itself, or dissolving, dissolving back into space." We need to know the status of things well, understanding what is erroneous and what is not and becoming able to dissolve these conceptions back into the sphere of reality.

Happiness comes through taming the mind; without taming the mind there is no way to be happy. The basis of this is a reasoned determination to be freed from cyclic existence. In the Buddhist scriptures it is explained that there is no beginning to the mind and hence no beginning to one's rebirths. In terms of reasoning, there is no way that consciousness can serve as a substantial cause of matter and no way that matter can serve as a substantial cause of consciousness. The only thing that can serve as a substantial cause of consciousness is a former consciousness. Through this reasoning, former and future lives are established.

Once there are future lifetimes, it can be decided that no matter how much prosperity and so forth you have in this lifetime—even if you are a billionaire—on the last day when you are dying you cannot take even one penny with you. No matter how many good friends you have, in the end you cannot take even one friend with you. What goes with you that is helpful is the strength of your own merit, your good deeds. Therefore, it is dangerous to be one hundred percent involved in affairs limited in perspective just to this lifetime. Although it would be impractical to put all of your time into deep matters that will help future lifetimes, it would be a good idea to put fifty percent of your energy into concerns for this lifetime and fifty percent into deeper topics. We have to live, we have a stomach which must be filled, but at maximum this life can be only around one hundred years and thus is short compared to future lifetimes. It is worthwhile to think of your future lives too and worthwhile to prepare for them, reducing a little the involvement of the mind just in the affairs of this lifetime.

Is it not the case that when we examine the marvels of cyclic existence, we find that they actually have the nature of suffering? They are not such that no matter how much we use them, they are always pleasurable. For example, if you have many houses, since you are only one person, when you use a particular house, the other houses remain empty. Then, when you go to another of the houses, this house is not much use. Similarly, even if you have a lot of money and stock up huge quantities of food, you have only one mouth and one stomach. You cannot eat more than one person's amount; if you ate enough for two, you would die. It is better right from the beginning to set limits and be content.

If you are not content but greedy, wanting this and wanting that, there is no way that all desires could be fulfilled. Even if you had control over all the world, it still would not be enough. Desire cannot be fulfilled. Moreover, when you are desiring, desiring, desiring, you face many obstacles, disappointments, unhappiness, and difficulties. Great desire not only knows no end but also itself creates trouble.

Pleasure and pain are effects. That pleasure and pain change indicates that they depend upon causes. Once they are caused, the happiness that you want is obtained through generating its causes, and the suffering that you do not want is removed through getting rid of its causes. If you have in your continuum a cause of suffering, even if you do not want that suffering, you will undergo it.

Since pleasure and pain are in a process of cause and effect, we can know what will come in the future in that future appearances depend upon the activities and thoughts we are engaged in now. Looked at this way, we can see that we are accumulating in every minute many karmas—actions— that will influence our rebirths in the future. Thus, it can be decided that if we do not utilize a method to bring about the end of the causes impelling the process of cyclic existence, there is no way to end suffering.

When we investigate it, our mental and physical aggregates which are under the influence of contaminated actions and afflictions are phenomena having a nature of suffering. The past causes of our aggregates are impure; in terms of their present entities, mind and body serve as bases of suffering; and in terms of the future they induce suffering to be experienced later.

In the beginning we experience suffering during birth and then during childhood. At the end of life, there is old age—becoming physically decrepit, unable to move, see, and hear well, with many discomforts and many pains—and finally the suffering of death. Between the sufferings of birth and death we are held by various types of suffering—such as sickness, not getting what we want, getting what we do not want. In this way, these aggregates of mind and body serve as a basis for suffering.

Is this teaching pessimistic? Not at all. As much as you recognize suffering so much do you make effort toward victory over suffering. For instance, you work hard five days in the week to get more pay for the sake of more comfort and so forth; also, you make great effort early in your life so that later you can live happily. For greater comfort you make a sacrifice.

As much as you can increase recognition of suffering, so much closer do you approach the state of liberation from that suffering. Therefore, you should not take delight in the possibility of assuming in future lifetimes this type of body and mind under the influence of contaminated actions and afflictive emotions. Rather, you should seek a state in which the aggregates that serve as the basis of suffering are completely extinguished. The expanse of reality into which the defilements inducing suffering have been extinguished is called liberation.

We should turn away not only from attraction to the appearances of this lifetime but also from attraction to the marvels of cyclic existence in future lifetimes since as long as we have these contaminated aggregates, there is no hope for real peace. Thinking thus on the disadvantages of cyclic existence, it is possible to develop a wish to get out of cyclic existence to a state of liberation.

When investigating this way, it is necessary to proceed by way of a union of analytical meditation and stabilizing meditation. First, analytically investigate the reasons behind the determination to leave cyclic existence, and then when some conviction develops, stabilize—without analyzing—on what you have understood. When your understanding begins to weaken, return to analytical meditation, then back to stabilizing meditation, and so forth.

What is the measure of having generated a fully qualified determination to leave cyclic existence after training in this way?

> *If, having meditated thus, you do not generate admiration*
> *Even for an instant for the prosperity of cyclic existence*
> *And if an attitude seeking liberation arises day and night,*
> *Then the thought definitely to leave cyclic existence has been generated.*

If, having overcome both the emphasis on the appearances of this life and attraction to the marvels of cyclic existence in general through repeated familiarization with these thoughts, you spontaneously and continuously seek to be freed from cyclic existence, without for a moment being distracted by attachment thinking from the depths, "This is wonderful," "I must have this," "Oh, if I only could have this," and so forth, you have then generated a fully qualified determination to be freed from cyclic existence.

This attitude, to be truly effective, must actually be implemented and not just verbalized. As Shāntideva says:[14]

> Would a sick person be helped
> Merely by reading a medical text?

It is not sufficient just to read about medicine, it must be taken internally in order to bring about a cure.

It is easy to lecture on the doctrine, or to hear it spoken, but hard to put it into practice. Without actually practicing the teachings, however, there is no way for good results to be produced. If the cause is only a verbal explanation, the effect cannot be anything more. When hungry, we need actual food; mere descriptions of tasty French or Chinese food cannot nourish us. As Buddha said, "I indicate the path of liberation to you; know that liberation itself depends upon you."

It may seem on first hearing them that these Buddhist ideas we have been discussing are unusual and perhaps impossible to achieve. However, as Shāntideva says:[15]

> There is nothing whatsoever that does not
> Become easier when one is accustomed to it.

There is nothing that cannot eventually be achieved once one has grown accustomed to it. All these states gradually can be generated, by growing familiar with them. The test of these teachings is to make effort at them over a long period of time. As Buddha says in a tantra [in paraphrase], "If you put into practice what I have said and it cannot be achieved, then what I have said is a lie." Therefore, at first it is necessary to practice and gain experience; in this way you will come to understand the truth of Buddha's teachings.

This completes the section on the generation of determination to be freed from cyclic existence: its causes, the methods for generating this determination, and the measure of its having been generated. The second of the three principal aspects of the path is the altruistic intention to become enlightened. As Tsongkhapa says, the determination to leave cyclic existence must be conjoined with the altruistic intention to become enlightened. Without the conjunction of these two aspects, their practice will not serve as a cause of becoming a Buddha; thus, the next stanza sets forth the reason for cultivating the altruistic attitude:

> *Also, if this thought definitely to leave cyclic existence*
> *Is not conjoined with generation of a complete aspiration to highest*
> *enlightenment,*

*It does not become a cause of the marvelous bliss of unsurpassed
  enlightenment.*
*Thus, the intelligent should generate the supreme altruistic intention
  to become enlightened.*

The altruistic intention to become enlightened, or mind of
enlightenment, is a special attitude of seeking your own full
enlightenment as a Buddha for the sake of sentient beings—the
welfare of sentient beings being your main object of intent. In
order to generate such an attitude, it is necessary to develop great
compassion observing sentient beings and wishing them to be free
from suffering and its causes. In order to generate that, it is necessary to reflect on the ways in which sentient beings suffer. This is
done through extending to others the type of realization of suffering that you develop with respect to yourself when cultivating
the determination to be freed from cyclic existence.

The next two stanzas describe the means for cultivating the
altruistic intention to become enlightened, first outlining the sufferings that are characteristic of cyclic existence:

*[All ordinary beings] are carried by the continuum of four
  powerful currents,*
*Are tied with the tight bonds of actions difficult to
  oppose,*
*Have entered into the iron cage of apprehending self
  [inherent existence],*
*Are completely beclouded with the thick darkness of
  ignorance,*
*Are born into cyclic existence limitlessly, and in their births
  Are tortured ceaselessly by the three sufferings.*
*Thinking thus of the condition of mothers who have come
  to such a state,*

Generate the supreme altruistic intention to become
  enlightened.

These thoughts are powerful and, if correctly applied to our own condition, can enhance the wish to leave cyclic existence. Then, by applying these realizations to the experiences of other sentient beings, compassion can be generated.

What is the meaning of being carried by the continuum of the four powerful currents? There are various explanations, but here the essential meaning is that all beings are overwhelmed by the four powerful currents of birth, aging, sickness, and death. Though we do not want these sufferings, we nevertheless undergo them; like being carried away by a great river, we are under their force. Our being powerlessly carried away by these four powerful river currents is the result of being tied with the tight bonds of our own previous actions and their predispositions that are difficult to oppose, and we are tied with these tight bonds because of being under the influence of afflictive emotions such as desire and hatred. Those are generated due to our having entered into the very hard, obstructive, and difficult to penetrate cage of the innate apprehension of an inherently existent "I" and "mine."

Observing our own "I," or self, we misconceive it to be inherently existent and through this misconception are drawn into afflictive emotions that motivate actions tying us in tight bonds and causing us to be swept away by the four powerful river currents of suffering. We are led into this faulty view of an inherently existent "I" by the force of the thick darkness of the misconception that other phenomena, primarily the mental and physical aggregates that are the basis of designation of the "I," inherently exist. Based on this, we generate the misconception that the "I" and "mine" inherently exist, whereupon the afflictive emotions of desire, hatred, and so forth are generated, causing us to engage in contaminated actions, thereby accumulating the karmas that bind us tightly.

Through such a causal process, beings come to be fettered with these mental and physical aggregates that have a nature of the sufferings of birth, aging, sickness, and death. Because of this causal sequence we undergo the three types of suffering: physical and mental pain, the suffering of change, and the pervasive suffering of conditioning which is merely to be under the influence of a contaminated process of causation. Analysis of this situation of suffering and the sources of suffering in relation to yourself helps to generate the determination to be freed from cyclic existence, whereas reflection on the countless others who were your mothers in former lifetimes and are endlessly tortured by such suffering evokes the generation of love, compassion, and the altruistic intention to become a Buddha in order to be of service to them. We ourselves want happiness and want to avoid suffering, and the same is true for all other sentient beings oppressed by the misery of cyclic existence. Those who suffer in this way lack the knowledge of what to adopt and what to discard in order to achieve happiness and avoid suffering. As Shāntideva says in his *Engaging in the Bodhisattva Deeds:*[16]

> Although [sentient beings] want to get rid of suffering,
> They manifestly run to suffering itself.
> Though they want happiness, out of confusion
> They destroy their own happiness like an enemy.

Though people do not want suffering, they rush toward it; though they want happiness, out of confusion they achieve the opposite.

To help sentient beings achieve liberation, we need to help them to understand the techniques for achieving happiness and removing suffering through identifying without error what to adopt and what to discard. Dharmakīrti's *Commentary on (Dignāga's) "Compilation of Prime Cognition"* says:[17]

> In order to overcome suffering [in others]
> The merciful engage in methods.
> When the causes of what arise from those methods are
>   obscure [to oneself],
> It is difficult to explain them [to others].

If you yourself do not know the topics needed in order to help others, there is nothing you can do. In order fully to bring about the welfare of other sentient beings it is necessary to know from a subtle level those things that will help others, the essential points of what to adopt and what to discard. Beyond this, you also need to know the dispositions, interests, and so forth of the sentient beings you seek to help. Thus, it is necessary to remove the obstructions to knowing all objects of knowledge. For, when all these obstructions have been removed, one has achieved the omniscience of a Buddha, the exalted wisdom knowing all aspects of objects of knowledge.

Since Bodhisattvas are seeking to help all sentient beings, they take as their main object of abandonment the obstructions to omniscience and work at the antidote to these obstructions. For, without knowing all, it is possible to help a small number of beings but impossible fully and effectively to help a vast number. This is why it is necessary to achieve Buddhahood in order to be of effective service to sentient beings.

Unable to bear the suffering of sentient beings without doing something about it, you generate strong compassion and love, wishing beings to be rid of suffering and to possess happiness. Then, seeing that to accomplish this purpose there is no way but to achieve Buddhahood, you generate the altruistic intention to achieve enlightenment. This intention to yourself attain the omniscience of a Buddha in order to be of service to others is called the altruistic mind of enlightenment (*bodhicitta, byang chub kyi sems*). It involves two aspirations—seeking the welfare of others through seeking your own enlightenment.

Based on the earlier description of the measure of having generated the determination to be freed from cyclic existence, we can understand the measure of having attained the altruistic mind of enlightenment; therefore, Tsongkhapa did not explicitly mention it. If, no matter what you are doing, in some portion of the mind there remains a constant intense wish for the welfare of sentient beings and a seeking of enlightenment for their sake, you have generated a fully qualified altruistic mind of enlightenment.

It is important to realize that our personalities are not suddenly and completely transformed as we try to develop such attitudes. Our natures, our characteristic dispositions, change only gradually. Differences are not seen at once, but over time. If we cultivate the altruistic intention to become enlightened slowly and steadily and, after five or ten years have passed, consider the changes that have occurred in our way of thinking and actions, the results of our efforts —the improvement—will be clearly discernible.

According to common sight, Shākyamuni Buddha spent six years practicing austerities and leading an ascetic life. He made this display of renouncing the pleasures of his household, becoming a monk, renouncing worldly facilities, going into ascetic retreat, and so forth in order to indicate the difficulties of the path his followers should pursue. How could it be that Buddha would have had to expend such tremendous effort to achieve realization and yet we could achieve the same realization quickly and without much effort? We cannot.

Having reached the point where a portion of the mind is continuously involved with the wish to achieve Buddhahood for the sake of all beings, you should conjoin this with the rite of aspirational mind generation for the sake of making it more stable. Also, it is necessary to train in the causes that will prevent deterioration of the aspirational mind in this or future lifetimes.

Then, it is not sufficient merely to generate the aspirational form of the mind of enlightenment; the practical mind of enlightenment must also be generated, for intention alone is not enough. You must come to understand that further training is necessary—the practice of the six perfections: giving, ethics, patience, effort, concentration, and wisdom. Having trained in the wish to engage in these practices, you take the Bodhisattva vows actually to do so.

If these vows are taken and the practice of the six perfections has gone well, it is then possible to receive initiation and engage in the practice of mantra [tantra]. This is the fully qualified mode of procedure set forth in the great books, undertaken when there is time and opportunity to progress in this way. Otherwise, as is now the widespread custom, when you have some understanding of the three principal aspects of the path—the determination to be freed from cyclic existence, the altruistic intention to become enlightened, and the correct view of emptiness—and are making great effort at developing these attitudes, it becomes possible to enter the practice of mantra. However, if you do not have understanding of the three principal aspects of the path, do not have faith from the depths of the heart in the Three Jewels [Buddha, his doctrine, and the spiritual community], and so forth, it would be extremely difficult to say that you have actually attained mantric initiation even if you have attended a ceremony.

The foundation of the altruistic mind of enlightenment is a good heart, a good mind, at all times. All of us can benefit from cultivating this; we should not get angry, fight, backbite, and so forth. When people engage in such activities, they do so for the sake of personal concerns but actually are only harming them-

selves. Therefore, all of us need to do whatever we can to cultivate a good mind, a good heart. I am not just explaining this; I, too,
am doing as much as I can to practice it. Everyone needs to do
whatever is possible, for as much as we can practice this, so much
will it help.

If you engage in such practices and gain experience of them,
your attitudes and way of viewing other people will change; then
when a problem—which you have encountered before—arises,
you will not respond with the same excitement as previously, will
not generate the same negative attitudes. This change is not from
something external, is not a matter of getting a new nose or a new
hairstyle, but takes place within the mind. Some people can withstand problems whereas others cannot; the difference is one of
internal attitude.

The change from putting these teachings into practice comes
slowly. After some time, we may encounter those who tell us we
have changed; this is a good sign that the practices have been
effective. Such response is welcome, for it indicates that we are no
longer bringing trouble to other people but are, instead, acting as
a good citizen of the world. You may not be able to levitate, fly,
or display similar feats, but such abilities are secondary and in fact
counterproductive if you are making trouble in the world. What
is important is to tame the mind, to learn to be a good person. If
we practice this teaching, nirvana will gradually come, but if we
act with bitterness and hatred, nirvana will only become more
distant.

The emphasis in Buddhism is on oneself, on the use we make
of this doctrine. Though Buddhist teachings offer the refuges of
Buddha, the doctrine, and the spiritual community, these are to
help us generate the power of our own practice. Among the three
refuges, the main refuge is the doctrine, not the doctrine within
someone else's continuum but that which we ourselves must gen-

erate in our own continuum. Without individual effort and practice, the Three Jewels of Buddha, the doctrine, and the spiritual community cannot provide any refuge.

This concludes the section of the altruistic intention to become enlightened; we have now reached the point of the last of the three principal aspects of the path, the correct view of emptiness. Why is it important to generate the wisdom realizing emptiness? Tsongkhapa says:

> *If you do not have the wisdom realizing the way things are,*
> *Even though you have developed the thought definitely to leave*
>   *cyclic existence and the altruistic intention,*
> *The root of cyclic existence cannot be cut.*
> *Therefore work at the means of realizing dependent-arising.*

"The way things are" refers to the mode of subsistence of phenomena, of which there are many levels. Here Tsongkhapa means the most subtle level, the final reality. Of the two truths, this is the ultimate truth. There are many conventional modes of subsistence, ways that phenomena abide, but the correct view of emptiness apprehends the final mode of subsistence, the ultimate truth.

Without the wisdom realizing the final mode of subsistence of phenomena, even though you have made great effort in meditation and have generated both the determination to be freed from cyclic existence and the altruistic intention to gain enlightenment, the root of cyclic existence still cannot be severed. For, the root of cyclic existence meets back to ignorance of the mode of subsistence of phenomena, misconception of the nature of persons and other phenomena. It is necessary to generate a wisdom consciousness that, within observing the same objects, has a mode of apprehension directly contradictory with that of this ignorant misconception. Even though the mere wish to leave cyclic existence or the mere altruistic intention to become enlightened indirectly help, they cannot serve as direct antidotes overcoming the misconception that is the root of cyclic existence. This is why the view realizing emptiness is needed.

Notice that Tsongkhapa exhorts us to "work at the means of realizing dependent-arising," not "work at the means of realizing emptiness." This is because the meaning of dependent-arising resides in the meaning of emptiness, and conversely, the meaning of emptiness resides in the meaning of dependent-arising. Therefore, in order to indicate that emptiness should be understood as the meaning of dependent-arising, and vice versa, thereby freeing one from the two extremes, he says that effort should be made at the means of realizing dependent-arising.

Emptiness should be understood not as a mere negation of everything but as a negation of inherent existence—the absence of which is compatible with dependent-arising. If the understanding of emptiness and the understanding of dependent-arising become unrelated and emptiness is misinterpreted as nihilism, not only would emptiness not be understood correctly but also such conception would, rather than being advantageous, have the great fault of falling to an extreme of annihilation. Therefore, Tsongkhapa explicitly speaks of understanding dependent-arising. Then:

Whoever, seeing the cause and effect of all phenomena
Of cyclic existence and nirvana as infallible,
Thoroughly destroys the mode of misapprehension of those objects
*   [as inherently existent]*
Has entered on a path pleasing to Buddha.

When, through investigating this final mode of subsistence of phenomena, we come to understand the non-existence of the ref-

Portrait of the Dalai Lama circa 1950s.

Photo: Brian Beresford
Collection/Nomad Pictures

Formal portrait from the 1950s.

Photographer unknown

Giving teachings, 1979.
Photo: Brian Beresford

Teaching on meditation
in Ithaca, New York,
October 1979.

Photographer unknown

Visiting a Buddhist center. *Location and photographer unknown*

Meeting with faculty and area leaders, including Onondaga Nation Chief Oren Lyons, Huston Smith, and Agehananda Bharati at Syracuse University in 1979. Photographer unknown.

His Holiness at a Senate Foreign Relations Committee luncheon in 1991, Washington, D.C. Photo: Sidney Piburn

Greeting children in Ithaca, New York. Photographer unknown

The Dalai Lama in Toronto in 1990. Photo: Chris Banigan

At the Wembley Conference Centre in London, England in 1993.
Photo: Brian Beresford

Giving teachings in Dharamsala, India. Photo: Alison Wright

The Dalai Lama meeting a young Tibetan girl, Dharamsala, India.
Photo: Alison Wright

At Breaker Bay, Wellington, New Zealand. Photo: *Jacqui Walker*

The Dalai Lama, Dehra Dun, India. Photo:Alison Wright

MCI Center, Washington, D.C., in 2005. Photo: Mitchell Layton

A talk at the Fleet Center in Boston, Massachusetts in 2003.
Photo: Alison Wright

erent object of the conception of self, or inherent existence, in persons or phenomena—that is, when we realize the absence of inherent existence—within still being able posit, without error, the cause and effect of all the phenomena included within cyclic existence and nirvana, at that time we have entered on the path that pleases Buddha. Emptiness is to be understood within not overriding your understanding of the cause and effect of mundane and supramundane phenomena, which obviously bring help and harm and cannot be denied. When emptiness is realized within understanding the non-mistakenness, non-confusion, and non-disordering of the process of cause and effect, that is to say, dependent-arising, this realization is capable of destroying all misapprehension of objects as inherently existent.

> As long as the two, realization of appearances—
>   the infallibility of dependent-arising—
> And the realization of emptiness—the non-assertion
>   [of inherent existence]—
> Seem to be separate, there is still no realization
> Of the thought of Shākyamuni Buddha.

If the understanding of appearances as unconfused dependent-arisings and the understanding of the emptiness of inherent existence of those appearances seem mutually exclusive, unrelated—if the understanding of the one does not facilitate understanding of the other or makes the other seem impossible—then you have not understood the thought of Shākyamuni Buddha. If it is the case that your realization of emptiness causes realization of dependent-arising to lessen or that your realization of dependent-arising causes realization of emptiness to lessen and these two realizations alternate as if separate and contradictory, you do not have the proper view.

Rather:

When [the two realizations exist] simultaneously without alternation
And when from only seeing dependent-arising as infallible,
Definite knowledge entirely destroys the mode of
 apprehension [of the conception of inherent existence],
Then the analysis of the view [of reality] is complete.

The wisdom realizing the lack of inherent existence, the absence of a self-instituting entity, is induced through searching for and not finding an object designated, for instance, one's own body, using a method of analysis such as the sevenfold reasoning.[18] Finally, through the reason of the subject's being a dependent-arising, the practitioner induces ascertainment that it is devoid of inherent existence. For, once it is under the influence of other factors, it depends upon them, and it is through its dependence on something else that the subject is shown to be empty of existing under its own power. In that we establish, through the reason of dependence on something else, or dependent-arising, that a subject is empty of existing under its own power, a dependently arisen phenomenon is left as positable after the refutation.

If we investigate a human who appears in a dream and an actual human of the waking state by way of the sevenfold reasoning, to an equal extent no self-instituting entity can be found in either case. However, although the dream human and the actual human, when investigated with the sevenfold reasoning, are equally unfindable, this does not mean that a dream human is to be posited as a human. Such would contradict valid cognition that experiences conventional objects; a subsequent conventional valid cognition refutes that a dream human is a human, whereas positing an actual human as a human is not damaged by conventional valid cognition.

Even though a human cannot be found when sought through

the sevenfold reasoning, it is unsuitable to conclude that humans do not exist, because that assertion would be refuted by conventional valid cognition. Conventional valid cognition establishes actual human beings, and, therefore, humans must be posited as existing. In that they are not findable under analysis such as the sevenfold reasoning but do exist, it can be decided that humans exist not by way of their own power but only under the influence of or in dependence upon other factors. In this way, the meaning of being empty of being under its own power comes to mean depending on others.

When Nāgārjuna and his students cite reasons proving the emptiness of phenomena, they often use the reason of dependent-arising, that phenomena are produced in dependence upon causes and conditions, and so forth. As Nāgārjuna says in his *Treatise on the Middle:*[19]

> Because there are no phenomena
> That are not dependent-arisings,
> There are no phenomena that are not
> Empty [of inherent existence].

Once there is no phenomenon that is not a dependent-arising, there is no phenomenon that is not empty of inherent existence. Āryadeva's *Four Hundred* says:[20]

> All these [phenomena] are not self-powered;
> Thus, there is no self [inherent existence].

No phenomenon exists under its own power; therefore, all phenomena are devoid of being established by way of their own character. As the reason why phenomena are empty, they did not say that objects are not seen, not touched, or not felt. Thus, when phenomena are said to be empty, this does not mean that they are empty of the capacity to perform functions but that they are empty of their own inherent existence.

Moreover, the meaning of dependent-arising is not that phenomena inherently arise in dependence upon causes and conditions, but that they arise in dependence upon causes and conditions like a magician's illusions. If you understand the meaning of emptiness and dependent-arising well, you can, with respect to one object, understand its inevitable unmistaken appearance as well as its emptiness of inherent existence; these two are not at all contradictory. Otherwise, you would think that it would be impossible to realize these two factors, the unfabricated reality of emptiness and the fabricated fact of dependent-arising, with respect to one object. However, once you have established the emptiness of inherent existence by the very reason of dependent-arising, it is impossible for the understanding of appearance and the understanding of emptiness to become separated.

An emptiness of inherent existence appears to the mind through the route of eliminating an object of negation, which in this case is inherent existence. At that time, a mere vacuity that is the negative of inherent existence appears to the mind; this is an absence that does not imply another positive phenomenon in its place. To understand emptiness it is necessary to eliminate an object of negation just as, for example, to understand the absence of flowers here in front of me it is necessary to eliminate the presence of flowers. When we speak of this vacuity that is a mere negation or negative of inherent existence, we are talking about the way in which emptiness appears to the mind—as a mere vacuity devoid of the object of negation. We are not saying that at that time there is no consciousness or person realizing emptiness, for in fact we are describing how this appears in meditation to the mind of the meditator.

In brief, by reason of the fact that phenomena are dependent-arisings—that they arise dependently—we establish that they are empty of inherent existence. Once dependent-arising is used as the reason for the emptiness of inherent existence, then with respect to one basis [or object] the practitioner conveniently avoids the two extremes of inherent existence and utter non-existence.

When emptiness is understood from the very perception of appearances themselves—from the very perception of dependent-arising itself—this understanding of appearance assists in understanding emptiness. When an understanding of emptiness is achieved through the reason of perceiving just dependent-arising without depending on any other type of reasoning such that the understanding of the one does not harm the understanding of the other but instead they mutually help each other and there is no need to alternate understanding of appearances and understanding of emptiness as if they were unrelated and separate, the analysis of the view is complete.

As Chandrakīrti says in his *Supplement to (Nāgārjuna's) "Treatise on the Middle"* (*madhyamakāvatāra, dbu ma la 'jug pa*):[21]

> [When] yogis do not find the existence of this [chariot],
> How could it be said that what does not exist in the seven
>   ways [inherently] exists?
> Through that, they easily enter also into suchness.
> Therefore, here the establishment of this [chariot] is to be
>   asserted in that way.

When sought for in the seven ways, phenomena cannot be found; yet, they are posited as being existent. This existence derives not from the object's own power but from the other-power of conceptuality. Hence, a thorough understanding of how phenomena are posited conventionally helps in gaining an understanding of their ultimate nature.

Prior to this deep level of realization, when you gain a little understanding of emptiness, you might wonder whether the activities of cause and effect, agent, activity, and object are possible within emptiness. At that time, consider an image in a mirror which, while being a mere reflection, is produced when certain conditions are met and disappears when those conditions cease— this being an example of the feasibility of functionality within absence of inherent existence. Or, contemplate your own experience of the obvious help and harm that come from the presence and absence of certain phenomena, thereby strengthening conviction in dependent-arising. If you start moving to the extreme of the reification of existence, reflect on emptiness. In other words, when you are tending toward the extreme of nihilism, reflect more on dependent-arising; then, when you begin to move toward the extreme of inherent existence, reflect more on emptiness. With such skillful alternation of reflecting on emptiness and on dependent-arising by means of a union of stabilizing and analytical meditation, your understanding of both dependent-arising and the emptiness of inherent existence will become deeper and deeper, and at a certain point your understanding of appearances and emptiness will become equal.

The text continues:

> *Further, the extreme of [inherent] existence is excluded [by knowledge of the nature] of appearances [existing only as nominal designations],*
> *And the extreme of [total] non-existence is excluded [by knowledge of the nature] of emptiness [as the absence of inherent existence and not the absence of nominal existence].*

Among all four Buddhist schools of tenets as well as, for instance, the Sāṃkhya and even the Nihilist schools, it is held to be true that the extreme of non-existence—mis-identification of what exists as not existing—is cleared away by appearance and the extreme of existence—mis-identifying what does not exist as existing—is cleared away by emptiness. However, according to the uncommon view of the Middle Way Consequence School, the opposite also holds true: by way of appearance the extreme of existence is avoided, and by way of emptiness the extreme of non-existence is avoided. This doctrine derives from the pivotal point that the meaning of dependent-arising is the meaning of emptiness and the meaning of emptiness is the meaning of dependent-arising.

The understanding of dependent-arising differs among the Mind-Only School, Middle Way Autonomy School, and the Middle Way Consequence School. The Mind-Only School posits the meaning of dependent-arising only in terms of compounded phenomena, those that arise from and are dependent upon causes and conditions. In the Middle Way Autonomy School, the meaning of dependent-arising is applied to all phenomena, permanent and impermanent, in that all phenomena depend on their parts. In the Middle Way Consequence School, dependent-arising is, in addition, explained as the arising or establishment of all phenomena in dependence on imputation or designation by conceptuality. The mutual compatibility of such dependent-arising and emptiness is to be understood.

In this vein, the text says:

> *If within emptiness the appearance of cause and effect is known,*
> *You will not be captivated by extreme views.*

When, from within the sphere of emptiness, cause and effect appear in dependence upon emptiness in the sense that dependent-arisings are feasible because of emptiness, it is as if the dependent-arisings of cause and effects appear from or are produced from emptiness. When in dependence upon emptiness you understand the feasibility of dependent-arising, you are released from the two extremes.

Thus, the understanding of emptiness itself helps you to avoid the extreme of non-existence. Also, when you understand that dependence upon causes and conditions, parts, or a designating consciousness contradicts inherent existence, that very understanding of dependent-arising will help you to avoid the extreme of over-reification of existence. Once the meaning of emptiness appears as dependent-arising such that what is just empty of inherent existence appears as cause and effect, it is impossible for the mind to be captivated by an extreme view reifying what does not exist or deprecating what does exist.

If this view of emptiness is practiced in conjunction with just the determination to be freed from cyclic existence, it will act as a cause of liberation from cyclic existence. If it is cultivated also in conjunction with the altruistic intention to become enlightened, it serves as a cause of full enlightenment as a Buddha. Since the view realizing emptiness is a common cause of the enlightenments of all three vehicles—the vehicles of Hearers, Solitary Realizers, and Bodhisattvas—it is compared to a mother.

The special practitioners of mantra for whom the mantra system was intentionally spoken must have as their view of reality the view of the Middle Way Consequence system. However, in general, it is not necessary to hold this view to be a practitioner of mantra; the philosophical view can be either Mind-Only or Middle Way. However, mantra cannot be practiced within a view lower than these; the coarse view of realizing only the selflessness of persons, as is set forth in the Great Exposition and Sūtra Schools, is not sufficient.

This completes the discussion of the three principal aspects of the path to enlightenment: the determination to be freed from cyclic existence, the altruistic intention to become enlightened, and the correct view of emptiness. It is primarily through the perfections of concentration and wisdom that the distinctive profundity of the greater power of mantra is found, with practice centered on these same three aspects.

The actual basis of practice is the altruistic intention to become enlightened, the determination to leave cyclic existence being a preparation for that. The six perfections are the topics of training of Bodhisattvas, and among them, the distinguishing features of mantra are concerned with the perfections of concentration and wisdom. Hence, all practices of all vehicles—small, great, and within the Great Vehicle, the sūtra and mantra systems—can be included within (1) the preparations, (2) the actual central part of the practices of Bodhisattvas, and (3) supplements to it.

Concluding the explanation of the three principal aspects of the path, Tsongkhapa gives advice that once we have understood the important points of the three aspects, these paths and their fruits must be generated within our own continuum:

> *When you have realized thus just as they are*
> *The essentials of the three principal aspects of the path,*
> *Resort to solitude and generate the power of effort.*
> *Accomplish quickly your final aim, my child.*

This is initially accomplished through hearing the teaching, then by way of the thinking which removes false superimpositions with respect to those topics and induces definite knowledge, and finally by meditation in which all distractions are removed and the mind is concentrated single-pointedly. In this way you should achieve the three principal aspects of the path and the fruit which they bring about, the omniscience of Buddhahood.

This concludes an explanatory transmission on the three principal aspects of the path, which are a great composite of practices, an excellent guide. In receiving such a transmission you also receive a blessing. If you train in these practices continuously, you will come to realize them.

It is essential to generate a good attitude, a good heart, as much as possible. From this, happiness in both the short term and the long term for both yourself and others will come.

SELF AND SELFLESSNESS

I AM VERY HAPPY to have the opportunity to speak at this famous university and especially to the Center for Study of World Religions. When I arrived, I felt an immediate warm feeling for all of you. A deeper human relation with each other is very important. Mere politeness and diplomacy are, of course, nice but cannot reach the depths. Openness, straightforwardness, and sincerity can reach more deeply.

If we want real harmony and friendship, first we must know each other. Knowledge is the basis, for without knowing each other it is difficult to build trust and to reach a state of genuine unity, without which it is hard to get peace. Heart-to-heart contact is essential. Nowadays, in some cases we are lacking real human relations; with this, we lose respect for the value of humanity, coming to regard human beings as if parts of a machine.

If we lose recognition of the value of human beings, it is extremely unfortunate. A human being is much more than just material—money and wealth. Wealth and money are meant for human benefit, not human beings for money. If we concentrate in an extreme way on wealth and external progress, neglecting human values and human dignity, the result will be unhappiness, mental unrest, discouragement, and depression.

If we realize, "I am a human being. A human being can do anything," this determination, courage, and self-confidence are important sources of victory and success. Without will power and determination, even something that you might have achieved easily cannot be achieved. If you have will power and reasonable courage—not blind courage but courage without pride—even things that seemed impossible at a certain stage turn into being possible because of continuing effort inspired by that courage. Thus, determination is important.

How can this be developed? Not through machines, not by money, but by our own inner strength based on clear realization of the value of human beings, of human dignity. For, once we realize that a human being is much more than just material, much more than just money, we can feel the importance of human life, from which we can feel the importance of compassion and kindness.

Human beings by nature want happiness and do not want suffering. With that feeling everyone tries to achieve happiness and tries to get rid of suffering, and everyone has the basic right to do this. In this way, all here are the same, whether rich or poor, educated or uneducated, Easterner or Westerner, believer or non-believer, and within believers whether Buddhist, Christian, Jewish, Muslim, and so on. Basically, from the viewpoint of real human value we are all the same.

For instance, I come from the East, more specifically, from Tibet. Materially, our general situation is very different from that in the United States, but if we look deeper, I am a human being, you are human beings—the same. If we go into deep space, from that perspective this small planet has no boundaries; there is just one planet. All these demarcations are artificially made. We fabricate distinctions based on color, geographical location, and so forth, and then on the basis of a feeling of separation, we sometimes quarrel with each other, sometimes criticize, and sometimes fight. From a broader viewpoint, however, we are all brothers and sisters.

Socially speaking, this type of attitude of valuing others is essential and, at the same time, it is beneficial in our own daily life; with it we can remain mentally calm, having much inner peace. Though in daily life not everything is successful—it being natural for some of our tasks to fail—we will not lose a sense of inner peace and stability. If you have a basic concern for others, even failure cannot disturb your mind.

Many problems are minimized because of inner attitude. Despite obstacles, you can remain in peace and calm, whereby the people you associate with can also share that calm and peaceful atmosphere. If, however, you become tense and angry, you yourself lose your inner peace and from strong emotions of anger and attachment, cannot sleep well and cannot eat even if good food is in front of you. You will do something; your family members and even your pets, dogs and cats, will suffer; you might even throw out your friends. As a result of anger and hatred there is no peace. We all know this from our own experience.

When truly considered, strong emotional feelings of anger and hatred are not at all good for your own happiness, and because they create a bad atmosphere, your neighbors, friends, and even parents are affected and become distant. Thus, for our own daily life and for society as a whole, our mental attitude is important.

As a result of highly developed science and technology, we are going deep into space. This is very good. From my childhood I have liked science and technology; they are absolutely necessary for human benefit. At the same time, if you look inside, though your head is not big, there is much space yet to explore. Thus, it would be worthwhile to direct half of our energy outside and half inside. Think more: Who am "I"? What is the nature of mind? What is the benefit of good thought? What is the benefit of bad thought? Make this sort of investigation. Think, think, think.

Through such thought, we can gain clear recognition that a certain part of our mind is a trouble-maker, worthwhile to control, whereas another part is beneficial for ourselves and others, worthwhile to increase. In this way, self-examination is valuable.

Though my experience as a Buddhist monk is not exalted, by my own little experience I can feel the benefit of these attitudes—love, compassion, recognition of human dignity, human value. Now at age forty-four, I have spent many years trying to develop compassion and kindness; I feel that as a result of these practices I am quite a happy person. Despite many difficult circumstances, I am happy. If because of these difficulties I always felt sad, I could not be effective since a sad person cannot influence reality. Still, accepting unfortunate events does not mean that one has to be discouraged. We are trying to overcome these difficulties and tragedies, yet remain peaceful and stable.

Out of my experience, I tell my friends, wherever I go, about the importance of love and compassion. Though the words are not elegant, they are meaningful and valuable. Further, it is easy to talk about love, compassion, and kindness, but the mere words are not effective. If you develop these attitudes and experience them, you will know their real value; so, it is worthwhile to try to develop them. If you agree, please try. If not, leave it.

Originally, I had no particular purpose in coming to this country except to exchange ideas, but the purpose has grown into the promotion of compassion and love as well as closer understanding between the various religions. Over the last few weeks I have had quite a few chances to meet with followers of different faiths. Certain basic motivations or basic points of all religions are the same—love, a sense of brotherhood and sisterhood, and an ultimate goal of the happiness of human society. The different, often opposing, philosophies are methods aimed at the same result. The main theme is the same. With respect and sincerity we can see that all religions are good—techniques through which different persons can gain peace.

I have only a few days left in my visit. I feel it has made some small contribution in the field of love, kindness, and unity; so I am happy.

The second part of my talk, being about the nature of self, is more technical; so, my English will say goodbye, and I will speak through an interpreter.

To cultivate compassion—altruism—in meditation it is necessary to have the assistance of wisdom. It is said that with the help of wisdom, compassion can become limitless. This is because afflictive emotions prevent the development of limitless compassion, and in order to destroy these afflictive emotions it is necessary to know the nature of phenomena. The reason for this is that the afflictive emotions superimpose a goodness and badness upon phenomena that exceeds the measure of what is there, the sign of this being that after we are either very desirous or very angry and that emotion has subsided, when we look at the same object, we see it entirely differently and even burst into laughter at ourselves. To counter this superimposition and hence prevent the arising of afflictive emotions it is necessary to know the final nature of phenomena correctly, without superimposition; we need to know the absence of inherent existence in all phenomena.

This mode of subsistence pervades all phenomena; however, due to the type of substratum or subject it is easier for this final nature to appear to the mind with respect to the person than it is with respect to other phenomena. Thus, it is important when first ascertaining the final status of things to initially settle the final status of the person. However, without ascertaining what the person is, it is impossible to understand the final nature or reality of the person.

Therefore, what is a person? What is the self? Buddhism asserts selflessness; is it not that self is non-existent? If Buddhists did assert that there are no persons and that selves are non-existent, there would not be anybody to meditate on selflessness, and there would be no one with respect to whom one could cultivate compassion. Hence, our own experience establishes that there are persons, selves.

If the self is established by experience, what is this theory of selflessness? Is this not a big contradiction? It is not. Let me explain. Analyze whether there is a difference between the way the "I" appears when you are relaxed and the way it appears when you are excited. For instance, if someone mistakenly accuses you, "You did such and such awful thing," and you feel, "I didn't do that," how does the "I" appear to your mind at that time? Similarly, when you take an enemy to mind, thinking, "This is my enemy," that enemy appears to your mind to exist in its own right in a self-instituting way as something concretely pointable with a finger.

Thus, phenomena appear to exist from their own side whereas, in fact, they do not. Their being established from their own side, their inherent establishment, is called "self"; its non-existence is "selflessness," and it is similarly true with respect to both persons (the other meaning of self) and other phenomena.

There are many different ways in which the person or "I" appears to our minds. In one way, the "I" appears to be permanent, unitary, and under its own power; in this mode of appearance the "I" seems to be a separate entity from mind and body with the person as the user or enjoyer and mind and body as what is used or enjoyed. No Buddhist school of tenets accepts that such a person exists; there are qualms about a couple of the sub-schools within the Great Exposition School that need to be eliminated, but otherwise there are none.

In another mode of appearance the "I" seems to have its own substantially existent or self-sufficient entity but to be of the same character as mind and body. There are both innate and artificial [or learned] forms of consciousnesses that conceive the "I" to exist in accordance with this appearance.

Again, in another mode of appearance, the "I" does not appear to exist ultimately but appears to exist by way of its own character conventionally. Another is the appearance of the "I" as if it exists inherently; our innate misconception of "I" is a consciousness that views the "I" in this last way as concretely existent in accordance with this appearance. This form of misconception exists in all beings, whether they have studied and been affected by a system or not.

Now, although all of these appear, in fact none of these exist. According to the various Buddhist systems, the non-existence of these respective levels of self, of reification, constitutes selflessness, progressing from the coarser to the subtler.

But then what is the conventionally existent "I" that undergoes help and harm? Within the Buddhist schools there are many different assertions on what the person who undergoes help and harm is. Some systems assert that consciousness is the person; others, the mental consciousness; others, a mind-basis-of-all (*ālaya-vijñāna, kun gzhi rnam shes*) which is separate from the mental consciousness. However, according to the most profound school of Buddhism, the Middle Way Consequence School, the person is merely designated in dependence upon the aggregates of mind and body. Also because, between mind and body, mind is more subtle and more continuous, the "I" or person is merely designated in dependence upon the continuum of consciousness.

Only this mere "I"—a dependently designated "I"—can be posited as that which, without any investigation and analysis, appears to an innate awareness when we think, "I am going," "I am staying," and so forth. Because it is dependently designated, it is dependent. Dependent and independent are explicitly contradictory, a dichotomy. For instance, although horse and human are mutually exclusive, they are not explicitly contradictory, a dichotomy, whereas human and non-human are. In the same way, dependent and independent are explicitly contradictory; anything considered has to be either the one or the other—there is no third category.

Because the "I" is dependently designated, there cannot be an independent "I" under its own power. This non-existence of an independent "I" under its own power is called the selflessness of the "I." Since this is the case, it is through the dependent nature of an existent basis, the "I," that one can speak of its selflessness. For this reason, when you understand selflessness well, you must have understood the existence of its basis. Since the dependence of a particular existent base is used as the reason why that base is empty of inherent existence, it can be easily seen that emptiness is not nihilism.

When the meaning of the emptiness of inherent existence appears in the context of dependent-arising, the extreme of utter non-existence is avoided. When dependent-arising is understood as the reason why something is empty of inherent existence, the extreme of the reification of existence is avoided. To ascertain the view of the middle way, it is necessary to be free from these two extremes of utter non-existence and reification of existence into inherent existence.

In this way, the various Buddhist systems of tenets identify in many different ways, coarser and subtler, the "I" that serves as the basis or substratum for ascertaining the nature of reality. The innate forms of false appearance, not involving investigation and analysis, occur even for small babies. A sign that the earlier levels of the appearance and misconception of self, both in innate and artificial ways, are more coarse and the latter ones more subtle is that even while you ascertain the non-existence of the earlier ones and the functioning of that ascertainment has not degenerated, the conception of self of the latter, more subtle varieties, can still operate. However, when you ascertain a subtler level of selflessness and the functioning of that ascertaining consciousness has not deteriorated, the coarser types of conceptions of self cannot operate at all.

To ascertain the meaning of selflessness, in general you must engage in analytical meditation, reflectively analyzing with reasoning. This is why in Nāgārjuna's *Treatise on the Middle* many reasonings are presented, all for the sake of proving from many viewpoints that all phenomena are empty of being established under their own power, empty of inherent existence. The *Kāshyapa Chapter Sūtra (kāśyapaparivarta, 'od srung gi le'u)* in the *Pile of Jewels Sūtra (ratnakūṭa, dkon brtsegs)*, in the context of presenting the three doors of liberation, says that, in brief, forms are not empty because of emptiness, forms themselves are empty. Therefore, emptiness does means not that a phenomenon is empty of being some other object but that it itself is empty of its own inherent existence. Thus, it is not an other-emptiness but a self-emptiness in that objects are empty of their own intrinsic establishment.

Similarly, the *Heart Sūtra* says, "Form is emptiness; emptiness is form." Taking form as the example, that form is emptiness means that the final nature of forms is their natural voidness of inherent existence; because forms are dependent-arisings, they are empty of an independent self-powered entity.

That emptiness is form means that this final nature, emptiness, which is the absence of a basic self-powered principle of these things which exist in the manner of depending on other factors— this natural voidness of inherent existence—makes possible the forms that are its sport in that they are established from it in dependence upon conditions. Since forms are those which are empty of true establishment—since forms are the bases of emptiness— emptiness is form; forms appear as like reflections of emptiness.

This final nature of forms, which is their absence of not depending on other factors, is the emptiness of forms, and thus forms are the sport of emptiness. Like the two sides of the hand, when looked at from this side, there is the emptiness of inherent existence, the final nature, but when looked at from the other side, there is the appearance that is the substratum of emptiness. They are one entity. Therefore, form is emptiness, and emptiness is form.

Contemplating the meaning of emptiness in this way, you gradually make progress over the paths. The progression is indicated in the mantra in the *Heart Sūtra: gate gate pāragate pārasaṃgate bodhi svāhā* (Proceed, proceed, proceed beyond, thoroughly proceed beyond, be founded in enlightenment.) The first *gate* refers to the path of accumulation; the second, to the path of preparation. Over these two periods you ascertain emptiness in the manner of dualistic appearance of the wisdom consciousness and the emptiness being realized. Then, "proceed beyond" (*pāragate*) indicates passing beyond the mundane level to the supramundane level of the path of seeing in which dualistic appearance has vanished. "Thoroughly proceed beyond" (*pārasaṃgate*) refers to the path of meditation during which you familiarize again and again with the emptiness that was first directly seen on the path of seeing. Through it, you finally pass beyond cyclic existence to the level of enlightenment (*bodhi*)—a state of being a source of help and happiness for all sentient beings.

Question: If there is no self, what goes from one lifetime to another?

Answer: The mere self or mere "I"—a self that does not inherently exist—goes from one lifetime to another. Also, even though consciousness is closely related with matter, consciousness is an entity of mere luminosity and knowing and thus cannot be produced from matter but must be produced in dependence upon a former moment of mere luminosity and knowing. Therefore, the continuum of consciousness also has no beginning and no end. The existent self or "I" is designated in dependence upon this continuum of mind. The self that is negated is inherent existence.

Question: What is the role of desire in the nature of the self?

Answer: There are two types of desires: false desires based on superimposition of what does not actually exist and desires based on reason. Desire generated by afflictive emotions creates a lot of trouble whereas reasoned desire can lead to liberation and omniscience. To sustain our lives day by day we must use reasoned desire and must control desires motivated by unreasoned afflictive emotions.

Question: Do you dream while sleeping?

Answer: Of course. For someone who is practicing yoga, there is much that can be done during dreams. First it is necessary to recognize a dream as a dream during the dream. You must have such experience yourselves.

In conclusion, there are many young students here, and the future depends upon the younger generation. Knowledge is important, but at the same time, more important than education is the mind implementing that education. If we use knowledge while lacking something in our hearts—if we use only the brain—we can bring more trouble and tragedy to human society. The human brain must be balanced with a good heart.

TIBETAN VIEWS ON DYING

THIS MORNING I visited the University of Virginia Medical Center where they work to prolong life. Later I spoke with Dr. Ian Stevenson about reincarnation—how people are reborn from a previous life. Now, I will speak on how we die, the process of dying and how to prepare for it.

Death, being unwanted, has been analyzed since the distant past both within and outside of religion. In Buddhism, the first of Buddha's teachings is that of the four noble truths, and from among the four truths, the first is that of true sufferings. It is important to recognize suffering. There are three types: the suffering of pain itself, the suffering of change, and the pervasive suffering of being under the influence of a contaminated process of conditioning. After you recognize suffering, you need to identify its causes and get rid of those causes. It is necessary to cultivate the path consciousnesses by which you achieve the cessation that is the extinguishment of the causes bringing about suffering. These are the four truths: sufferings, the sources of suffering, the cessation of suffering and its causes, and the paths that bring about such cessation.

The four truths are divided into sixteen attributes, four for each truth. The four attributes of true sufferings are impermanence, suffering, emptiness, and selflessness. Within the topic of impermanence, there are two types—coarse impermanence and subtle impermanence. Subtle impermanence refers to something that scientists who take an interest in minute particles can describe because they are not just taking for granted the appearance of a solid object such as a table, which seems to be the one that was here yesterday, but look at the changes within the smaller elements that compose objects. The substances composing these external objects disintegrate moment by moment; similarly, the internal consciousnesses observing those external objects also disintegrate moment by moment. This momentary disintegration is subtle impermanence. Coarse impermanence is, for instance, the destruction of an object, or in terms of people, it is a person's death.

There are great benefits to being mindful of death. As I said before, if suffering is recognized, its causes can be researched, and, above all, it can be faced, confronted. Sooner or later death will come. We do not want it, but once we are under the influence of contaminated actions and afflictive emotions, it will definitely come. If right from the beginning you think about death and prepare fully, such preparation can help when death actually comes. This is the purpose of becoming mindful of death.

What I am explaining here is helped by the explanations of rebirth given by Dr. Ian Stevenson of your University.[22] How? If you believe just in this life and do not accept its continuation, it does not matter much whether you are mindful of death or not. Meditation on death and impermanence is based on the theory of the continuation of a consciousness in rebirth. Once there is another lifetime—a continuation of consciousness in rebirth—it can only be helpful to prepare for death since, if prepared, you will most likely not be anxious and frightened by the process of dying, not complicating the situation with your own thought.

If there are future lifetimes, the quality of the next lifetime depends upon this lifetime. If you conduct your life now in a good manner, this will be beneficial to the next one. Anger, attachment, and so forth cause us not to conduct our lives in a favorable manner, leading to harmful results in the future, and a cause of generating these unfavorable states of mind is the conception of permanence. There are other causes such as the conception of the inherent existence of objects, but when you are able now to decrease the degree of the conception of permanence, attachment to this lifetime becomes weaker. Also, when you are able to keep impermanence in mind—seeing that the very nature of things is that they disintegrate—most likely you will not be greatly shocked by death when it actually comes.

To overcome death entirely, it is necessary to end your own afflictive emotions. For by overcoming the afflictive emotions, birth ceases, and thus death ceases also. To do this, it is necessary to make effort, and to generate that exertion it helps to reflect on death and impermanence. From thinking on death and impermanence, you generate an attitude of not wanting such, this in turn drawing you into investigating techniques for overcoming death.

Also, through reflecting on death and impermanence, your concern solely with superficial matters limited in scope just to this lifetime will diminish in strength. Death will definitely come. If you spend your life overly concerned with just the temporary affairs of this lifetime, and make no preparation for it, then on the day when it comes, you will be unable to think about anything except your own mental suffering and fear and will have no opportunity to practice anything else. This can produce a sense of regret. However, if you have reflected frequently on death and impermanence, you know that such will come, and you will make preparation at an easy pace with plenty of time. Then when death actually comes, it will be easier. Still, I have heard from a few hospital workers that some who have no concern about a future life die more easily than some religious persons who worry about the next lifetime.

Since the mind at the time of dying is a proximate cause of the continuation into the next lifetime, it is important to use the mind near the time of death in practice. No matter what has happened in terms of good and bad within this particular lifetime, what happens right around the time of death is particularly powerful. Therefore, it is important to learn about the process of dying and prepare for it.

Within the Bodhisattva Vehicle and specifically in the Mantra [or Tantra] Vehicle, there are explanations that correlate the three types of bodies—Truth Body, Complete Enjoyment Body, and Emanation Body—that a Buddha has in the effect stage with three types of processes that we naturally have in the ordinary state—death, intermediate state, and rebirth. Three paths are presented by which these ordinary factors, which correspond in rough form to enlightenment factors, can be used. In these explanations unique to Highest Yoga Mantra, it is also said that knowledge of the process of dying is extremely important.

In terms of how to prepare for death, in Buddhism there are explanations found in sūtra and mantra, and within mantra, explanations according to the three lower tantras—Action, Performance, and Yoga Tantra—as well as according to Highest Yoga Tantra. What is the entity or nature of death? It is the finishing or ending of life. In Vasubandhu's *Treasury of Manifest Knowledge,* life is said to serve as a basis of warmth and consciousness, whereby death is the ending of that function. Thus, while this temporary, coarse body and consciousness are together, one is alive, and when they separate, that is death. It is necessary to distinguish between coarse, subtle, and very subtle body and mind; death is the separation of consciousness from the coarse body as there is no way for the most subtle consciousness to separate from the most subtle physical level, the latter being just the wind, or inner energy, on which that consciousness is mounted.

Different conditions of dying are described. One is to die when the lifespan has been exhausted; another, to die when your merit has been consumed, and the third is to die in an accident. The latter would be a case, for instance, of drinking, getting drunk, driving, and killing yourself on the highway.

A vague indication appears near the time of death as to what kind of rebirth you will be taking. This is seen in how the warmth gathers within the body. For some people the warmth begins gathering, or withdrawing, from the upper part of the body, and for others it starts to withdraw first from the bottom part. It is worse for the warmth to start gathering from the top down and better for it to gather from the bottom up.

Some people die peacefully; others die within great fright. To the person who is dying, various appearances, pleasant and unpleasant, dawn to the mind.

In terms of explaining the process of death from the point of view of the mantric system, in Highest Yoga Tantra death is explained as the cessation of coarse winds or energies. Since death is related with the cessation of inner energies and these inner energies depend upon the body, a knowledge of the structure of the body is important. In the mantric system, the topics that are mainly explained here are those of the channels, inner winds, and drops of essential fluid. In the sūtra system, eighty thousand channels are set forth whereas in the mantric system there are seventy-two thousand. From among these, three are most important—the central channel running from the forehead to the top of the head and down to the base of the spine with channels on its right and left sides. In terms of the internal winds or energies, many different types are explained, but ten are most important—five main and five secondary winds. The essential drops are the red and white constituents. In general, beings die similarly in the sense that the process is culminated by the dawning of the clear light of death; however, due to various types of coursings in the channels by these inner winds and drops, different types of appearances occur to a dying person. Also, because of minor physical differences the process differs slightly from person to person.

In the stages of dying, twenty-five factors are said to dissolve. These are called the twenty-five gross objects:

Five aggregates:
forms, feelings, discriminations, compositional factors, and consciousnesses
Four constituents:
the four elements of earth, water, fire, and wind
Six sources:
the eye sense, ear sense, nose sense, tongue sense, body sense, and mental sense
Five objects:
visible forms, sounds, odors, tastes, and touches
Five ordinary wisdoms:
basic mirror-like wisdom, basic wisdom of equality, basic wisdom of analysis, basic wisdom of achieving activities, and basic wisdom of the nature of phenomena.

During the actual process of dying, these factors dissolve in stages. Marking these stages are different external physical signs as well as internal signs. For these signs to occur gradually and in order, the constituents of the dying person must not have been overly consumed by disease, and the person must not have died suddenly in an accident. If you die in an accident on the highway, these eight stages will dawn quickly, and you will not have a chance to practice anything, suffering the double loss of accidental death before your time and of not having a chance to practice in conjunction with the gradual unfolding of the stages of dissolution. If you die naturally, the signs will appear gradually in order.

The first stage is represented by the dissolution of the aggregate of forms. In rough terms, when the aggregate of forms begins to disintegrate, this means that the earth constituent is losing its force in the sense of becoming less capable of serving as a basis of consciousness. Simultaneous with this, the capacity of the water constituent in your body to serve as a basis of consciousness becomes more manifest; this process is called "dissolution of the earth constituent into the water constituent." As an external sign of this, your limbs become thinner, more frail, and the freshness of your appearance deteriorates. You have the sense that your body is sinking under the ground, and your eyesight becomes unclear.

At this time, the internal sign, according to the *Guhyasamāja Tantra,* is that you have a visual sense of seeing a mirage. However, according to the *Kālachakra Tantra,* you have a visionary sense of smoke. This variance in explanation arises from slight differences in the physical structure of the channels, winds, and drops of essential fluid in the respective trainees of those tantras, specifically in the number of channel petals at the channel wheels at the top of the head and at the throat, for instance. Both of these tantras describe six channel centers in extensive form and four in brief form but differ with respect to the number of channel petals.

After that, in the second stage, the aggregate of feelings dissolves. At that time, the water constituent decreases in force in terms of its capacity to act as a basis of consciousness, due to which that capacity of the fire constituent [the factor of heat in the body] becomes more manifest. As external signs, the fluids of the body dry—your mouth dries, the fluid in the eyes dries a little, and your eyes move less. According to the *Guhyasamāja Tantra,* internally, the sign of this stage is that you have a sense of seeing an appearance of smoke.

In the third stage the aggregate of discriminations dissolves, at which time the fire constituent lessens in force in the sense that it is less able to serve as a basis of consciousness, the wind constituent thereby becoming manifest in terms of this capacity. As an external sign, your sense of heat diminishes, the heat of your body having become withdrawn; in terms of your own thought, your memory of the affairs of close persons deteriorates. As an internal sign you have a sense of an appearance of fireflies or scattering sparks.

In the fourth stage the aggregate of compositional factors dissolves, at which time the capacity of the wind constituent to act as a basis of consciousness weakens. As an external sign, your breath ceases. As an internal sign, you have a sense of a burning reddish glow from a flame; previously there were many appearances like fireflies and so forth, which become more and more subtle, leaving just a reddish glow. In general, people consider this to be death because your heart is no longer beating and you are no longer breathing. If doctors came, they would say you were already dead; however, from our point of view, you are still in the process of dying; you have not yet died. Your sense consciousnesses have disappeared, but the mental consciousness remains. However, this does not mean that you could revive.

Within the mental consciousness there are many levels of coarseness and subtlety. In Buddhist texts there are assertions of different numbers of consciousnesses—nine, eight, six, and one— although the most prevalent assertion is of six consciousnesses. The Mind-Only School Following Scripture asserts eight—the five sense consciousnesses, the mental consciousness, an afflicted mentality, and a mind-basis-of-all. The latter two terms are also used in other contexts with different meanings; thus, the usage of those terms does not necessarily involve an assertion of eight consciousnesses in accordance with this Mind-Only School.

Beyond mere number, consciousness can also be divided into main minds and mental factors, the former being the mere knower of the entity of an object and the latter being that which differentiates the features of the object. The general character of consciousness is mere luminosity and knowing, which pervades all consciousnesses. Its entity is mere luminosity, unobstructed by anything; its function is to know based on the appearance of whatsoever object.

In the production of a visual sense consciousness, for instance, three conditions are needed—an empowering condition which is a physical sense faculty; an observed-object-condition which here is a visible form, a color or shape; and an immediately preceding condition, a former moment of consciousness. When these three are complete, a consciousness apprehending a visible form is produced. The three conditions have different functions; the fact that the consciousness is an entity of luminosity and knowing is due to the immediately preceding condition; that it apprehends visible form and not sound is due to the empowering condition, the eye sense faculty; that it is generated in the image of a color or shape is due to the observed-object-condition, the object itself. This is how a coarse consciousness is produced.

Here, however, during the process of dying the bases of these coarse sense consciousnesses—the eye sense faculty, ear sense faculty, and so forth—have deteriorated, on account of which the consciousnesses associated with them cease. Still, there are four levels of grossness and subtlety within the minds that remain, and thus there are four further stages of dissolution of consciousness after the earlier four stages of dissolution of the elements. The coarser begin to dissolve first, starting with the eighty conceptual thoughts.[23] These eighty conceptions are divided into three groups, respectively characterizing the next three subtler levels of mind. Thirty-three have the nature of the mind of vivid white appearance; forty have the nature of the mind of vivid red increase; and seven have the nature of the mind of vivid black near-attainment. The level of fluctuation—great, middling, and small—of the inner wind or energy that is the mount of these three groups of conceptions serves to illustrate the nature of the movement of the wind or energy associated with the three subtler levels of mind.

When the eighty conceptual thoughts together with the winds or energies that serve as their mounts dissolve, the internal sign is that a white appearance dawns; this is the mind of vivid white appearance. It is compared to a clear autumn sky filled with just moonlight. There are no more external signs.

When the mind of vivid white appearance dissolves together with the wind or energy that serves as its mount, a more subtle mind appears, this one being called the mind of vivid red increase. It is compared to a clear autumn sky filled with just reddish or orange sunlight.

When the mind of vivid red increase dissolves along with its mount, a still more subtle mind appears, this being the mind of vivid black near-attainment. It is compared to the complete darkness of a clear autumn sky in the first period of the night. During the initial part of this level of mind, you are still aware, but then the capacity for conscious awareness deteriorates, and you become as if unconscious.

When the mind of vivid black near-attainment dissolves together with the wind that serves as its mount, the most subtle of all minds appears—the clear light of death, actual death. It is compared to an immaculate dawn sky in autumn, without any other appearance. The mind of clear light is called the fundamental mind because it is the root of all minds; in relation to it, all other minds are just adventitious. It is this mind that exists beginninglessly and continuously in each individual through each lifetime and into Buddhahood. An explanation of this is given only in Highest Yoga Mantra.

During the phases of dissolution, it is important to be aware; as much as you are aware, so much greater is the capacity to remember the previous life after rebirth. This is like the fact that if at night before going to sleep we strongly determine with clear awareness what time we want to rise in the morning and what we are going to do after rising, then even if while asleep we are not remembering this, due to the previous intentionality we rise right at that time and immediately remember what we are to do. In the same way, during these phases of dying, as long as awareness remains, you should take care to maintain its capacity in full alertness.

A person who dies naturally within physical well-being and without much physical deterioration will remain in the state of this subtlest mind, the mind of clear light, for about three days. During this time the subtlest consciousness still resides in the old body. Some exceptional people, who through practice during their lifetime have been able to identify the nature of mind and have engaged in practices concerned with the channels, winds, and drops, are able to recognize the process of death such that the clear light dawns within maintaining full awareness. Due to their control, they can remain in this state for a week or even a month according to their own wish. About ten instances of this have occurred among Tibetans since our arrival in India in 1959. Even in the hot season in India people have remained in the clear light for two weeks like someone asleep—no longer breathing, like a corpse but, unlike a corpse, not smelling.

When within that subtle mind of clear light there is a very slight movement, the mind of clear light ceases, the consciousness exits from the old body, and you begin the reverse process, going back into the mind of vivid black near-attainment and the other six levels of appearance—vivid red increase, vivid white appearance, appearance like a burning butter lamp, appearance like fireflies, appearance like smoke, and appearance like a mirage. If you are to be reborn in the Desire Realm or Form Realm these being rebirths requiring an intermediate state (*antarābhava, bar do*), at the time of the mind of black near-attainment the intermediate state begins. If you are to be reborn in the Formless Realm, there is no intermediate state.

For those who pass through an intermediate state, it ends with the connection to the new life state, at which time you pass again through the eight signs of death culminating in the dawning of the mind of clear light of death. If you are taking rebirth in a womb, the connection to the new life in the mother's womb and the dawning of the mind of black near-attainment after the clear light of the death of the intermediate state are simultaneous; thus, in a certain sense, a life begins with the mind of clear light.

Generally speaking, the ordinary life state is involved in the grossest level of consciousness; death, in the subtlest level; and the intermediate state, in a middle level. Similarly, within the twenty-four hour period of a day, the ordinary waking state is on the grossest level of consciousness; deep sleep, the subtlest level; and the dream state, in an intermediary level. Again, when a person faints, the mind becomes more subtle. Thus, in an ordinary day we pass through these various levels of mind though not in the full manner of the process of dying.

In conclusion, it is essential to identify your own basic mind, the mind of clear light. To realize the subtlest mind, the first step is realization of the nature of mind on the conventional level. With realization of the nature of mind you can concentrate on mind itself, gradually increasing the power of realization of the entity of consciousness. Through that method, the mind can be controlled. The strength of control, in turn, helps to stop coarse minds, and once those are stopped, subtler minds will automatically manifest. If, before death, you can realize the subtle mind, this subtle mind can be transformed into wisdom—the strongest weapon to destroy ignorance and the suffering it induces. For a practitioner there is much to be learned and much training to be done.

Question: Your Holiness said that part of the process of preparing for death is learning to experience the various signs of dying while still alive such that when you experience them at the time of death you are more prepared for them. Is there a practice by which the consciousness is separated from this coarse body during life, and do you see any parallel between this and experiences reported in West of people who come close to death and sense themselves as being outside of their physical body and inside another, more subtle body?

Answer: There are cases of coarse body and mind separating due to familiarization with such practices in former lifetimes whereby it appears to be a "gift" in this life, and there are also cases due to practice in this lifetime. Specifically, a special dream body is not just an appearance of the mind but an actual subtle body that can separate from the usual body and can experience external facts just as we normally do. I cannot say in detail whether the usual body keeps breathing or passes into a state like that of deep meditation in which the coarse breath ceases. In any case, the subtle body can go anywhere. Also, since without a coarse physical body you are not restricted by distance, you can go into deep space, can reach everywhere. Then, you can return to the old body according to your wish. This can occur in near-death experiences as well as at a time of severe illness.

Question: Many of us have read the *Tibetan Book of the Dead* and are suitably impressed by the peaceful and wrathful deities one is to meet in the intermediate state, but we are not, by and large, in Tibetan Buddhism and have not received initiations and permissions, nor instructions on the meditations. Would those of us who have no idea beforehand of how these deities look still see the same figures in this state?

Answer: I do not think so. Generally speaking, the *Tibetan Book of the Dead* describes appearances of peaceful and wrathful deities for one who has practiced and become familiar with these while alive. If a practitioner is unable to be liberated through recognition and usage of the states prior to dying, then at each period in the intermediate state a practitioner of the *Tibetan Book of the Dead* is seeking to cause appearances of peaceful and wrathful deities to occur in accordance with predetermined practice. Through practicing so that they will appear, the practitioner is seeking to become aware during the intermediate state so as to be able to identify the entity of basic knowledge, basic mind, the luminous and knowing nature of the mind—this being a practice of the Nyingma system of the Great Completeness. The power of one's previous familiarity with these deities serves to spark mindfulness such that, as the appearances gradually occur, one gets various chances to succeed at awakening awareness and, thereby, realization of the ultimate nature of the mind.

Question: Please explain more about *rig pa* (fundamental mind or basic knowledge) in terms of daily life.

Answer: There is a time when one's basic mind has been generated into a conscious entity but apprehensions have not yet set in. It is important to identify this factor of clear knowing. Yogis who have experience with this have said that in order to do this, faith and respect for the doctrine are very important and that it is necessary to receive instructions from a lama that are based on his or her own experience. Until you have gained identification of this basic nature of the mind, it is difficult to experience. However, it helps if each day we look into our own minds and analyze what the basic character and nature of the mind is, this luminous and knowing nature. It is helpful to do this early in the morning because consciousness is clearer at that time.

Question: Do you feel that it is proper or effective for Westerners to use the *Tibetan Book of the Dead,* in translation, for dying persons even though they have not been instructed formally in the technique, and will it help the deceased if the requisite purity is present in the reader?

Answer: In general, without the preparation of initiation, meditation, and so forth, this would be difficult. It is necessary to be familiar with the teachings. Thus, if a dying person is familiar with the texts on the process of death, it is helpful to use them. Generally speaking, when a person is dying, it is important that he or she leave in a peaceful manner. One should not generate excitement or nervousness in a dying person. One should not act in such a way as to stir up the person; also from the viewpoint of the person who is dying, it is necessary to have clear thought.

Question: How is the strength of awareness increased?

Answer: Before the coarse consciousnesses dissolve, you need to generate powerful alertness. In meditation you should become familiar with similitudes of the states leading to death. In my daily practice, I meditatively pass through the stages of dying six or seven times. Whether I will succeed is yet to be seen, but at least I am achieving the causes of success by stimulating mindfulness and recognition. For instance, if you were going to engage in war in a certain area, you would study a map identifying where the mountain is, where the stream is, where the lake is, and so forth such that when you actually arrive there, you are able to identify what you are seeing and know what you are to do. Because beforehand you gained firm familiarity with what would appear, you do not shrink from the task or become anxious.

TRANSFORMING THE MIND THROUGH MEDITATION

NAROPA INSTITUTE, BOULDER, AND UNIVERSITY
OF COLORADO, DENVER

MEDITATION is a familiarization of the mind with an object of meditation. In terms of how the mind is familiarized with the object, there are many types of meditation. In one type, the mind is generated into the entity of a particular type of consciousness, as in meditating compassion or meditating wisdom. In such meditation you are seeking to generate your own mind into a compassionate consciousness or a wisdom consciousness—compassion and wisdom not being the object on which you are meditating, but the entity into which you are seeking to transform your consciousness through a process of familiarization.

However, when you meditate on impermanence or on selflessness, impermanence and selflessness are taken as the objects of the mode of apprehension of the mind, and you are meditating on them. In another type of meditation, if you meditate on the good qualities of a Buddha wishing to attain them, these qualities are objects of wishing; this is called meditation in the manner of wishing. Then, another type of meditation is one in which you cause levels of the path to appear to the mind in the sense of taking to mind that there are such and such levels of realization; this is called reflective meditation.

In another way, meditation is divided into two types: analytical and stabilizing. In general, calm abiding (*śamatha, zhi gnas*) is stabilizing meditation, whereas special insight (*vipaśyanā, lhag mthong*) is analytical meditation.

With respect to objects of meditation, the objects of both stabilizing and analytical meditation can be either the final mode of being of phenomena or any among the varieties of phenomena. In general, emptiness is something found at the conclusion of analysis by reasoning investigating the final mode of being of objects; nevertheless, at the time of stabilizing meditation observing emptiness, the meditator fixes one-pointedly on the meaning of emptiness that has been ascertained and does not analyze. Thus, there is both stabilizing and analytical meditation observing emptiness. Similarly, both stabilizing and analytical meditation observing any of the varieties of phenomena can occur depending on how the mind is acting on the object.

Calm abiding, which is predominantly stabilizing meditation, is common to both non-Buddhist and Buddhists. Within Buddhism it is common to both the Hearer and Great Vehicles, and within the Great Vehicle is common to both the Sūtra and Mantra Vehicles. I will explain in brief how to achieve calm abiding.

Our mind, as it is now, is completely scattered to external objects, due to which it is powerless. Our thought is like water running in every direction. But just as water, when channeled, becomes powerful, so it is with our minds.

How is the mind channeled? In the Mantra Vehicle in general and in Highest Yoga Mantra in particular, many techniques are described, but first I will describe the technique that is common to all vehicles. In order to set the mind steadily on an object of observation, it is necessary initially to identify an object of observation. Buddha described four types—objects for purifying behavior, skillful objects, objects for purifying afflictions, and pervasive objects. For example, with regard to objects for purifying behavior, no matter what afflictive emotion we predominantly engaged in earlier, its force remains with our mind now, and thus it is necessary to choose an object for meditation that will counter the force of this particular afflictive emotion. For someone who predominantly engaged in desire, the object of meditation is ugliness. From among the four mindful establishments this is explained in connection with mindful establishment on the body. Here, "ugliness" does not necessarily refer to distorted forms; the very nature of our body—composed of blood, flesh, bone, and so forth—might seem superficially to be beautiful with a good color, solid and yet soft to touch, but when it is investigated, you see that its essence is things like bone. If I were wearing X-ray glasses, I would see a room full of skeletons as well as a skeleton that is talking from this podium. Thus, meditating on "ugliness" means to investigate the nature of our physical body.

For someone who has predominantly engaged in hatred, the object of meditation is love. For someone who was predominantly sunk in obscuration, the meditation is on the twelve links of the dependent-arising of cyclic existence. For someone whose predominant afflictive emotion is pride, the meditation should be on the divisions of the constituents because, when meditating on the many divisions, you get to the point where you realize that there are many things you do not know, thereby lessening pride. For those dominated by conceptuality, the prescribed meditation is on observing the exhalation and inhalation of the breath. Those are the objects for purifying behavior.

As mentioned earlier, the object of observation could also be emptiness. Also, you could take even a flower, and so forth, as the object. Still another is to take your own mind as the object of observation. Also, a Buddhist could meditate on Buddha's body; a Christian could meditate on Jesus or the cross.

No matter what the object is, this is not a case of meditating within looking at an external object with your eyes but of causing an image of it to appear to the mental consciousness. This image is called a "reflection," and it is the object of observation.

Having identified the object, how do you set your mind on it? Initially, you have to hear about the object of meditation from a teacher; then, you gain ascertainment of it by thinking again and again on it. For instance, if you are to meditate on the body of a Buddha, first you need to come to know it through hearing it described or looking at a picture or statue and then get used to it so that it can appear clearly to the mind.

At that point, imagine it about four feet in front of you, at the height of your eyebrows. It should be meditated as clear, with a nature of light; this helps to prevent the onset of laxity.

Also, consider the imagined Buddha body to be heavy; this helps to prevent excitement. As much as you can reduce the size of the object, so much does it help in withdrawing the mind, channeling it. Your physical posture (see p. 80) is also important.

For the object of observation it is also possible to use letters or drops of light at important places in the body. When meditating this way, the object must be tiny; the smaller the object is, the better. Once the object originally has been determined, you may not change its size, bigger or smaller; you must consider it to have been fixed for the duration of generating calm abiding.

First cause the object to appear to the mind. Then, hold it with mindfulness such that you do not lose it. Not losing the object through mindfulness acts as a cause of developing introspection.

While keeping on the object, your mind must have two qualities—(1) great clarity not only of the object but also in the consciousness and (2) abiding one-pointedly on the object of observation. Two opposing factors prevent these from developing—laxity and excitement. Laxity prevents the development of clarity, and excitement prevents the stability of staying with the object.

Laxity is a case of the mind's becoming too relaxed, too loose, lacking intensity—the tautness of the mind having become weak. A cause of laxity is lethargy, which is like having a hat on the head, a heaviness. As an antidote, you have to make the mind more taut.

When the mode of apprehension of the mind is tightened, there is less danger of laxity but more danger of generating excitement. Scatterings of the mind that are due to desire are called excitement; thus, scattering can be to any type of object, whereas excitement is a scattering only to objects of desire. As an antidote to excitement and any other type of scattering, you need to lower the level of the mode of apprehension of the mind, making it less taut.

While holding the object of observation with mindfulness, investigate with introspection from time to time to see whether the mind has come under the influence of laxity or excitement. If through introspection you find that there is danger of laxity, you need to heighten the mode of apprehension; if there is danger of excitement, lower the mode of apprehension a little. Through experience, a sense of a moderate level of tautness of the mind will develop.

To heighten the level of the mode of apprehension of the mind, reflect on something that makes you joyous; to lower it, reflect on something that sobers the mind, such as suffering. When initially training this way, it is best to do frequent, short sessions of meditation, and because it is difficult initially to generate a deep state of meditation when in a busy, noisy city, you need complete isolation and tranquility. Without quiet, it is almost impossible to achieve a fully qualified state of calm abiding.

As you practice in this way, the mind gradually develops more and more stability, culminating in calm abiding. Through the power of stabilizing meditation in which the mind is set one-pointedly on its object of observation, mental pliancy is generated. In dependence upon that, physical pliancy is generated, leading to the bliss of physical pliancy. In dependence upon that, the bliss of mental pliancy is generated. At the point at which the bliss of mental pliancy becomes stable, calm abiding is attained. Among the four concentrations and four formless absorptions, this state—which is conjoined with physical and mental bliss—is the initial preparation for the first concentration.

Special insight is attained in a similar way when the bliss of mental pliancy is induced, not by the power of stabilizing meditation, but by the power of analysis with investigatory wisdom. There are mundane and supramundane forms of special insight. The mundane is a case of viewing a lower level as gross and a higher level as peaceful, whereas supramundane special insight, if taken in a general way, has the aspect of the four noble truths. From the specific viewpoint of the Great Vehicle systems of tenets, supramundane special insight has the aspect of the selflessness of phenomena.

To induce meditative stabilization even faster, the mantra systems have special techniques revolving around deity yoga. The path of deity yoga brings about speedier progress to Buddhahood through special techniques for developing unified concentration and wisdom, these being the last two of the six perfections—giving, ethics, patience, effort, concentration, and wisdom—which are described in the Bodhisattva scriptural collections. If you do not have concentration in which the mind is unfluctuatingly stable and clear, the faculty of wisdom cannot know its object, just as it is, in all its subtleties. Therefore, it is necessary to have concentration. The reason for cultivating wisdom realizing the emptiness of inherent existence is that even though you have mere concentration, it cannot harm the misconception that objects exist in and of themselves. A union of concentration and wisdom is needed.

According to the *Vajrapañjara Tantra,* an explanatory tantra of the Guhyasamāja cycle, there are four divisions of the Mantra Vehicle—Action, Performance, Yoga, and Highest Yoga Tantras. Among these, the three lower tantras—Action, Performance, and Yoga—describe a mode of progressing on the spiritual path in terms of yogas with and without signs, these both being yogas of the non-duality of the profound and the manifest. Meditative stabilization is achieved within taking—as the object of observation of the meditation—the clear appearance of your own body as the body of a deity. While observing your body clarified, or visualized, as a deity's body, you ascertain its absence of inherent existence, thus making a combination of manifestation in divine form and profound wisdom realizing the final nature of that body. Such profound realization and simultaneous divine appearance is the yoga of the non-duality of the profound and the manifest.

In Action Tantra during the yoga with signs the mode of generating or imagining yourself as a deity is by way of six steps called the six deities. The first is the ultimate deity, meditation on the emptiness of inherent existence equally of yourself and of the deity. The second is the sound deity, viewing an appearance of the natural form of emptiness as the reverberating sounds of the mantra of the particular deity in space.

The third is the letter deity in which the sounds of the mantra appear in the form of letters standing around the edge of a flat moon disc. The fourth is the form deity, a transformation of the moon and letters into the body of the deity.

The fifth is the seal deity, the blessing of important places of the divine body with hand gestures called "seals." Then, you set a white *oṃ* at the crown of the head, a red *āḥ* in the throat, and a blue *hūṃ* at the heart, symbolizing exalted body, speech, and mind, and concentrate on this divine body, which now has all the qualifications or signs of a deity. This is the last step, the sign deity.

When some success is gained in visualizing yourself as a deity, the concentrations of abiding in fire and abiding in sound are used to enhance speedy development of meditative stabilization. After that, you cultivate the yoga without signs, the concentration bestowing liberation at the end of sound. This is cultivation of supramundane special insight observing the emptiness of inherent existence. Although deity yoga is still done, the main emphasis is on the factor of ascertaining the final nature of phenomena.[24]

The explanation of the procedure of the path in Performance Tantra is roughly the same as in Action Tantra, but in Yoga Tantra it is slightly different. There, the bases of purification are explained as body, speech, mind, and activities, and as means of purification four seals are described for transforming these into the exalted body, speech, mind, and activities of the effect stage of Buddhahood. In this process the achievement of calm abiding is enhanced by meditation on a tiny hand symbol, such as a vajra, at the point of the nose, gradually increasing in number such that first your own body and then the surroundings are pervaded by the tiny hand symbols. The specific hand symbol is determined in accordance with the five Buddha lineages, the deities of which carry a special symbol in their hands; Vairochana, for instance, carries a wheel, Akṣhobhya a vajra. Meditation on such a tiny hand symbol helps in developing calm abiding due to the size of the object and helps in increasing meditative dexterity through the practice of dispersing and gathering many forms of the symbol.[25]

Highest Yoga Tantras mainly explain a yoga of undifferentiable bliss and emptiness in terms of two stages of yoga—a stage of generation, which is imaginary and fabricated, and a completion stage, which is non-imaginary and non-fabricated. In both the stage of generation and the completion stage in Highest Yoga Mantra the ordinary states of death, intermediate state, and rebirth are brought into the path to be transformed into the Three Bodies of a Buddha—Truth Body, Complete Enjoyment Body, and Emanation Body.

In Highest Yoga Mantra there are techniques for meditating on the inner channels, winds [energies], and drops of essential fluid. Presentations of the channels are given in two ways: one is a physical description, whereas the other is merely for meditation. The latter description is for the sake of specific meditative effects, and thus exact physical correspondence is not the aim. The sought after effects, however, are definitely produced.

A practitioner meditates on drops, light, or letters in these channel centers. Due to the special places where these are meditated and due to the force of initiation as well as of preliminary meditations called "approximation to the state of a deity," and so forth, just stabilizing meditation is used in cultivating special insight realizing the emptiness of inherent existence. Also, it is possible to achieve calm abiding and special insight simultaneously.

The technique of focusing on letters or light at important places within the body serves as a means of forcefully stopping conceptuality. The reason for stopping conceptuality is that within consciousness there are many levels from the gross to the most subtle, and in Highest Yoga Mantra the subtler levels of consciousness are transformed into path consciousnesses of wisdom. Normally, when we die, the grosser levels of consciousness cease, and the subtler levels become manifest, culminating in manifestation of the subtlest consciousness, the mind of clear light of death. An ordinary person has no awareness during this phase, being as if in a swoon. However, if while the body—the basis of the mind—has not degenerated a yogi withdraws the grosser levels of consciousness through the power of meditation, the subtler consciousnesses can be experienced in full awareness and clarity. Forcefully withdrawing the grosser and subtler levels of wind [energy] and mind, the yogi manifests the most subtle level, the mind of clear light.

Used in the path process, this level of consciousness is particularly powerful and quick. To ripen the mind so that these levels of the path can be practiced, it is necessary first to practice the stage of generation.

That is a just a brief presentation; understanding these states and how they are achieved in sūtra and mantra is very useful.

THE TWO TRUTHS

UNIVERSITY OF CALIFORNIA, BERKELEY

THERE ARE MANY different ways in which the basic structure of Buddhist doctrine can be presented. From one of the more important viewpoints, the bases are the two truths—conventional and ultimate; the paths which depend upon them, method and wisdom; and the fruits of those paths, the two Buddha Bodies—Form Bodies for the sake of helping others and the Truth Body which is the fulfillment of one's own welfare. In Buddhism there is no particular Buddha who was always a Buddha, who has been beginninglessly enlightened. Buddhas are beings who, like ourselves, originally had minds accompanied by defilements and stage by stage removed those defilements to the point where they transformed themselves into beings who had attained all good attributes and removed all faults.

The root of their ability to do this is the fact that the nature of the mind is mere luminosity and knowing. Mind is something that has the capacity of appearing in the aspect of whatsoever object through the force of the object's casting its aspect to it and is an entity of mere clarity and cognition, with a nature of experience. It disintegrates moment by moment. However, among its many causes—classified into substantial cause and cooperative conditions—it must, as an entity of conscious experience, have as its substantial cause an immediately preceding cause which is a former moment of consciousness. It is not possible for an entity with the character of luminosity and knowing to be produced from external material elements as its substantial cause. Similarly, an internal mind cannot act as the substantial cause of external elements. Since each moment of consciousness requires a former moment of consciousness as its substantial cause, there is no way but to posit that the basic continuum of mind is beginningless. Some specific types of minds [such as desire for an automobile] have a beginning and end, whereas other types [such as the ignorance conceiving inherent existence] have, in terms of their continuum, no beginning but an end. However, neither a beginning nor an end can be posited to the mind of luminosity and knowing. Therefore, although mind disintegrates moment by moment, its continuum is beginningless.

This being the situation of the mind, how is it transformed? That the mind has faulty states is due to ignorance, obscuration with respect to the mode of subsistence of phenomena. To remove this ignorance, it is necessary to generate knowledge of that mode of subsistence. To generate such a consciousness knowing the nature of phenomena, it is necessary to understand the objects that are to be known. With regard to what is to be known, there are two statuses—conventional objects that are mere appearances and the final mode of being of those objects. The former are objects found by consciousnesses distinguishing conventionalities, whereas the latter are objects found by consciousnesses distinguishing the final mode of subsistence. The first are called conventional truths (*saṃvṛtisatya, kun rdzob bden pa*), and the second are called ultimate truths (*paramārthasatya, don dam bden pa*).

Doctrines of the two truths are taught in different ways in non-Buddhist systems as well as in all the upper and lower Buddhist systems of tenets. Within Buddhism, some systems do and others do not assert a selflessness of phenomena; here I will not explain the assertions of the two schools—the Great Exposition School and the Sūtra School—which do not assert a selflessness of phenomena but will explain briefly the assertions on the two truths by the Mind-Only School and the Middle Way School, which assert a selflessness of phenomena.

In connection with the two truths as explained in the Mind-Only School, there is a presentation of the three natures. Other-powered or dependent natures (*paratantrasvabhāva, gzhan dbang gi rang bzhin*) are the substrata; imputational natures (*parikalpitasvabhāva, kun btags pa'i rang bzhin*) are the objects of negation that are negated with respect to those other-powered natures; and thoroughly established natures (*pariniṣpannasvabhāva, yongs su grub pa'i rang bzhin*) are the other-powered natures' emptiness of the imputational natures. Thoroughly established natures are emptinesses of a difference of entity between subject and object; they are ultimate truths.

In the Mind-Only School, each and every phenomenon is the same entity as the awareness perceiving it; there are no objects that are entities external to the consciousness perceiving them. Thus, in this system the term "self" in the view of selflessness is identified as external objects existing as different entities from the mind perceiving them; this is the final imputational nature of which phenomena are empty, which phenomena lack. Phenomena's emptiness of such "self" is the thoroughly established nature. Hence, the Mind-Only School asserts that all phenomena are as if exhausted within mind.

Within the Middle Way School scholars explain the two truths in various ways, but here I will describe mainly the assertion of Buddhapālita. He explains forms, sounds, and so forth, not as of the entity of the mind as the Mind-Only School does, but as different entities from the mind. Further, Buddhapālita explains that not only are these phenomena established as different entities from the mind perceiving them but also the mode of establishment of their entities is not as the Mind-Only School says. Rather, their entities are without inherent or true establishment.

Then, what is this absence of inherent or true establishment in Buddhapālita's system? It is best understood by explaining its opposite, inherent establishment or inherent existence. Whatever phenomena appear to us appear to exist objectively in their own right, in and of themselves. Though they appear to exist from their own side, when we analyze to determine whether they exist as they appear, we cannot find them under analysis. When an object is divided into its parts, the whole cannot be found—there is no way to posit the whole under analysis.

Furthermore, there is nothing among objects of knowledge that is partless. All physical objects have directional parts; for example, even when we consider the quarks that comprise the protons in a nucleus, they occupy a certain area and thus have directional parts. In his *Thirty Stanzas* (*triṃśikā, sum cu pa*) the Mind-Only scholar Vasubandhu analyzes at considerable length to show that even the most minute particle must have parts associated with the directions corresponding to the other particles surrounding it; he thereby demonstrates that there are no partless things.

Vasubandhu concludes—from proving that there are no partless things—that external objects do not exist. Using the reason that external objects are not found under analysis, he concludes that they do not exist. For the Middle Way School, however, even though partless particles do not exist at all, the mere fact that external objects are not found under analysis means that external objects are not truly established, not that they do not exist. Thus, not to be found under ultimate analysis means not to be truly existent, not non-existent.

Phenomena exist; that help and harm obviously come from them is a sign that they exist. However, they are empty of existing in the way in which they appear to us. That phenomena cannot be found under ultimate analysis indicates that they are not truly or inherently existent.

Once phenomena are empty of existing in the concrete manner in which they appear, all phenomena exist within the context and nature of an emptiness of inherent existence. For instance, within non-investigation and non-analysis we are using this lectern; a consciousness that, without investigation or analysis, thinks, "A lectern is here," is an awareness distinguishing a conventionality, and the object found by this consciousness, the mere lectern, is a conventional truth.

Still, if you are not satisfied with the mere appearance of the lectern but search to discover the status of its nature, the status of its entity, it cannot be found. Upon separating out the color, shape, and so forth that constitute the qualifications for a lectern and are in this way the substratum of the lectern that depends upon them, you cannot find the lectern.

The awareness or consciousness that searches in this way due to not being satisfied with the mere appearance of the object, the mere convention, is one concerned with the final nature of the object. What does this awareness find upon its analysis? It finds the non-finding of the lectern. When you search for the lectern—when the lectern is the substrate of the analysis—the non-finding of the lectern is the final nature of the lectern. It is a quality, the ultimate quality, of the object, and is the final mode of being, the mode of subsistence, of the object.

Thus, when Buddhapālita sets forth this doctrine of emptiness, he says not that phenomena are empty of the ability to perform functions but rather that phenomena are dependent-arisings and therefore empty of inherent existence. To be dependent on another and not to be dependent on another are explicitly contradictory; they are a dichotomy such that if something is not one of those two, it must be the other, and if it is established as one of those two, it cannot be the other. An example is human and non-human; anything is necessarily either human or non-human, and nothing is both. Although, for example, human and horse are contradictory, they are not explicitly contradictory, not a dichotomy. However, human and non-human are explicitly contradictory, a dichotomy; no third category that is neither of those two can be posited. Since the dependent and the independent are explicitly contradictory, once something is dependent, it is empty of being independent.

To speak about how this emptiness appears to the mind, it is necessary first to discuss consciousness. All objects of comprehension are included in the two truths, and the consciousnesses comprehending those objects are of many levels. There are those that realize obvious objects without depending on signs and reasonings; these are called directly perceiving consciousnesses. Others, in dependence upon signs or reasonings, realize an object that is not obvious; they are inferential consciousnesses.

With respect to the signs or reasons used in the process of inference, Dharmakīrti sets forth three main divisions: effect signs, nature signs, and signs of non-observation. Signs of non-observation are of two types—non-observation of the non-appearing and non-observation of what would be suitable to appear [if it did exist].[26] Among the latter are signs proving the absence of inherent existence, such as the unfindability of a phenomenon among or separate from its bases of designation. Based on such a reason, valid cognition of the emptiness of inherent existence is induced.

In conjunction with such a reasoning, one first states consequences (prasaṅga, thal 'gyur) to overcome the vibrancy of fixed wrong conceptions. Also, according to the Consequence School, consequences themselves can induce valid cognition of a thesis. In any case, in dependence on such proofs, one settles the absence of inherent existence of all phenomena, the mode of subsistence of phenomena, the ultimate truth.

The emptiness of inherent existence of an object ascertained in this way is a negative phenomenon from the division of all phenomena into positive and negative phenomena. Whether a phenomenon is positive or negative is determined not just by way of the word that expresses it but by way of how it appears to a conceptual consciousness apprehending it. For instance, the word "emptiness" is a negative word, and emptiness is a negative phenomenon. However, although the word "reality" (*dharmatā, chos nyid*) is not a negative word, when its meaning appears to the mind it must appear by way of a negative route—by way of explicitly eliminating an object of negation, inherent existence—and thus it is a negative phenomenon.

Among these negative phenomena, which appear to the mind through explicitly eliminating an object of negation, there are two types—those that imply something in place of the negation of their respective object of negation and those that do not. The former are called affirming negatives and the latter non-affirming negatives. In the case of an ultimate truth, an emptiness, when it appears as an object of the mind, only a mere vacuity that is the negation of its object of negation, inherent existence, appears; no positive phenomenon is implied in place of the negated object. Therefore, an ultimate truth, or emptiness, is a non-affirming negative.

This means that to a mind decisively realizing from the depths this non-affirming negative, the object of apprehension is just this elimination of the object of negation—just this absence of inherent existence. As long as the mode of apprehension does not deteriorate, only an utter vacuity that is the absence of inherent existence appears.

When you have had this experience in meditative equipoise, in the period subsequent to meditative equipoise although, as before, phenomena appear to exist inherently, the power of having ascertained the emptiness of inherent existence generates ascertainment such that you think that these phenomena are like illusions in that although they appear to exist inherently they do not. Furthermore, since desire, hatred, and so forth are produced with the assistance of the conception of inherent existence, the perception of phenomena as like illusions in that there is a conflict between the way they appear to inherently exist and the way they actually exist serves to control these unfavorable afflictive consciousnesses. This same perception also helps salutary virtuous consciousness, since in general they do not require the misconception of phenomena as inherently existent to operate.

In dependence on ultimate truths wisdom is developed, and in dependence upon conventional truths compassion and kindness toward others is meditated. These two, wisdom and compassion, must be practiced in union; this is the path of the union of wisdom and method.

In order to enhance the wisdom consciousness, the wisdoms arisen from hearing and thinking are not sufficient; the wisdom arisen from meditation must be generated. A wisdom consciousness observing emptiness that is a state arisen from meditation is itself a meditative stabilization that is a union of calm abiding and special insight. In addition, many special techniques are described in tantra for enhancing the development of this consciousness. The main technique is for one consciousness to contain the two factors of observing a mandala circle of deities and of simultaneously realizing their emptiness of inherent existence. In this way, the vast—the appearance of deities—and the profound—the realization of suchness—are complete in one consciousness.

The imprint, or result, of practicing this tantric yoga in which compassionate method and profound wisdom are combined in one consciousness is generation of the two Buddha Bodies. The Form Body—the physical manifestation of a Buddha—is the imprint of the yoga of imagining the divine circle that is related with conventional truths. The Truth Body—the exalted mind of a Buddha—is the imprint of the wisdom consciousness realizing emptiness, the ultimate truth. The root of the capacity for developing the Form and Truth Bodies of a Buddha is the very subtle wind [or energy] and very subtle consciousness which we have in our continuums now. This is called the Buddha nature.

Question: In Highest Yoga Tantra there is a practice of observing emptiness in meditation in conjunction with bliss. What is the purpose of this bliss?

Answer: In order to have a subtle consciousness ascertaining emptiness, it is necessary to stop the coarser levels of consciousness. When a blissful consciousness is generated, our awareness becomes more subtle; thus, the strongest level of bliss is used to assist the process of stopping the coarser levels of consciousness. That blissful consciousness itself then realizes the emptiness of inherent existence.[27]

Union of the Old and New Translation Schools

Union of the Modern and the Ancient, Boonesville, Virginia

THIS IS MORE OR LESS a personal account.

For a long time I have had the one-pointed belief that Nyingma, Sakya, Kagyu, and Geluk are all unions of sūtra and mantra as well as being of the Consequence School in terms of the view of emptiness. Therefore, I have had hope and interest in coming to know the various styles of explaining the view, meditation, and behavior in these schools and have made effort in this regard.

Even though in India there was no talk of old and new systems, in Tibet the presentations of mantra came to be divided into the Old and the New Translation Mantra Schools in dependence upon periods of translation of the scriptures. Nyingma is the Old; Sakya, Kagyu, and Geluk are included in the New, being those that arose subsequent to the translations of Rinchen Sangpo (*rin chen bzang po*, 958-1055).[28]

The newer schools do not differ to any significant degree among themselves with respect to the sūtra systems, but with respect to mantra [also called tantra] they differ slightly. When not investigated in detail, differences in terminology and so forth might lead one to think that there are great differences among the

New Translation Schools about the practice of mantra; however, their basic structure is the same.

The Kagyu lineage stems from Dakpo Hlarje (*dag po lha rje,* 1079-1153), his lama Milarepa (*mi la ras pa,* 1040-1123), and Milarepa's lama, Marpa (*mar pa,* 1012-1096). Marpa's main personal deity was Guhyasamāja in a lineage transmitted from Nāropa. Similarly, in the Geluk order Tsongkhapa's (*tsong kha pa,* 1357-1419) teaching on the five stages in the completion stage within Highest Yoga Tantra has as its source the teachings of Marpa's transmission of Nāropa's quintessential instructions on the *Guhyasamāja Tantra.* In addition, many other important topics in both the Kagyu and Geluk Schools such as the *Chakrasaṃvara Tantra,* long-life achievement, the *Hevajra Tantra,* and transference of consciousness stem from Marpa. Thus, the basis and over-all structure of the Kagyu and Geluk presentations of tantra are mostly the same, though the clarity and length of explanation sometimes differ.

With respect to philosophical view, the Translator Marpa explored the view of emptiness under the direction of Maitrīpāda, who in his *Ten Stanzas on Suchness* (*tattvadaśaka, de kho na nyid bcu pa*) says:[29]

> Not Aspectarians, not Non-Aspectarians,
> Even Proponents of the Middle who are not adorned
> With the guru's speech are only mediocre.

He says that both True and False Aspectarian Proponents of Mind-Only do not have the final view and that even within the Middle Way School, those who are not adorned with the quintessential instructions of the guru are mediocre. In commentary on this, Maitrīpāda's student, Sahajavajra, identifies the "guru" as the glorious Chandrakīrti, making it clear that Maitrīpāda considers

Chandrakīrti's quintessential instructions to be essential if the view is to be supreme. Thus, Maitrīpāda's view, and hence Marpa's, is that of Chandrakīrti's Middle Way Consequence School.

Furthermore, Marpa's student, Milarepa, in his "Song to the Five Long Life Sisters" *(tshe ring mched lnga)*[30] says that even though Buddhas, the Truth Body, grounds, paths, and so forth—even emptiness—do not ultimately exist, within the scope of non-analysis and non-investigation the omniscient Buddha said that everything exists for a conventional consciousness. Thus, Milarepa advocated a non-confusion of dependent-arisings in the sphere of conventional truths as well as the non-findability of even emptiness ultimately. In differentiating the two truths this way, Milarepa set forth the true, unmistaken view of the Middle Way Consequence School. Since the Geluk view is also of the Middle Way Consequence School, Kagyu and Geluk do not differ with respect to their philosophical view.

The Sakya School differs slightly in emphasis and in choice of terminology, but the general structure and systematic development are essentially the same. For instance, Kedrup [one of the two chief students of Tsongkhapa, founder of Geluk,] notes in his Miscellaneous Works that though the modes of explanation of the Middle Way view by Tsongkhapa and Rendawa *(red mda' ba,* 1349-1412), Tsongkhapa's Sakya teacher, differ, they are getting at the same thing. The mode of expression differs but not their basic thought. Thus, for the most part, it is easy to realize that the basic thought of Kagyu, Sakya, and Geluk is the same with respect to the philosophical view in that they all are of the Middle Way Consequence School.

The school in which it is difficult to see such similarity is the Old Translation School of Nyingma. In rough terms, practices can be divided into those of view, behavior, and meditation. Between the Old and New Translation Schools there is not much difference concerning behavior and meditation, with small but insignificant variations in the mode of teaching ranging from rites to the presentation of the path. However, the philosophical views, looked at superficially, might seem to vary to a greater degree due to the usage of different terminology.

That the very roots of Nyingma are valid and accord with reality was recognized even by Tsongkhapa, who received teachings on the Nyingma doctrine of the Great Completeness from the great adept from Hlodrak, Namkha Gyeltsen (*lho brag grub chen nam mkha' rgyal mtshan,* 1326-1401). Tsongkhapa took this Nyingma master as one of his lamas and praised his teaching; rather than go to India to settle points of the view, Tsongkhapa generated great ascertainment concerning the view through him. That he did so is clear from Tsongkhapa's biographies.[31]

Indeed, prior to the development of the New Translation Schools, there were many great scholars and adepts such as the twenty-five disciples of the precious master Padmasambhava—King Trisong Detsen (*khri srong lde brtsan,* b.742), and so forth—who ascended to the level of adept in their very lifetimes in dependence only on the Nyingma path. The New Translation Schools had not even formed then. Nowadays also, one sees many who show signs of having achieved great spiritual heights through following the Nyingma path. Thus, it can be decided that the Great Completeness of Nyingma is definitely a pure system of the profound practice of Highest Yoga Mantra.

In Kedrup's Miscellaneous Works a question is raised about deprecation of the Nyingma doctrine of the Great Completeness, the questioner wondering if it is a pure doctrine. In answer, Kedrup states that deprecation of the Old Translation doctrine of the Great Completeness has arisen from the outward behavior of some māntrikas [tantrists] who practice the Great Completeness. He points out that the Great Completeness is a practice of high levels of Highest Yoga Mantra and that in following this view many have obviously proceeded to high states of adepthood. He adds that Tibetan translators visiting India saw the original Sanskrit manuscripts of the *Secret Matrix Tantra* (*guhyagarbha, gsang ba'i snying po*) and so forth in Magadha and concludes that deprecation of this doctrine would cause rebirth in a bad transmigration. The passage in Kedrup's Miscellaneous Works reads:[32]

Question: This Old Translation School of Secret Mantra was refuted by earlier scholars, and there are also many nowadays who deprecate it. How is this?

Answer: The translations of the teachings of Secret Mantra during the earlier dissemination are called Old (*rnying ma*), and the translations during the later dissemination are called New (*gsar ma*). The reason for the frequent deprecation of the Old is that during the interstice when the teaching faded due to [King] Langdarma (*glang dar ma*, c. 803-842), māntrikas engaged in untoward behavior such as "union and release."[33] Also, nowadays there are many householder practitioners with hair coiled [in the style of a lay māntrika]. Derision of [Nyingma] doctrine seems to have arisen due to inferences based on these persons' behavior.

The actual situation regarding this Old Translation School of mantra is quite different. Initially the excellent religious kings sent translators who were reliable beings such as Vairochana and Ma and Nyek,[34] the five monks, and so forth with scoops of gold as offerings [to India]. There, they received doctrines of unsurpassed Secret Mantra such as the Great Completeness from persons indisputably renowned as scholars and adepts and then translated them. Moreover, Padmasambhava, Vimalamitra, Buddhaguhya, and others were

invited to Tibet where they set forth teachings of the profound doctrines belonging to the highest vehicle. It is established by valid cognition that through practicing these
systems an innumerable number were released [from cyclic
existence] and gained adepthood.

Also, in Samye (*bsam yas*) Monastery there still remain
many copies of Indian texts of the Old Translation School,
and Tibetan translators who went to India reported that
Indian editions of the *Secret Matrix Tantra,* the Five Scriptural
Sūtras (*lung gi mdo lnga*) and so forth exist in Magadha. Therefore, those who deprecate such profound doctrines of the
highest Great Vehicle are only [accumulating] the causes of
[rebirth in] a hell.

In this way, Kedrup identifies the Great Completeness as a unique
and most profound mode of practicing Highest Yoga Tantra.
Therefore, we can indeed conclude that it is a pure doctrine.

Many in the four main schools of Tibetan Buddhism—Nyingma, Sakya, Kagyu, and Geluk—have said that all four have the
same basic thought. In the Geluk School, the First Panchen Lama,
Losang Chökyi Gyeltsen (*blo bzang chos kyi rgyal mtshan,* 1567[?]-
1662), states in the root text to his text on the Great Seal that
although the schools use different verbal designations, when an
experienced yogi analyzes these, they all come down to the same
thought. The First Panchen Lama says:[35]

> Though there are many different designations of names
> [In the systems] of innate union, the small case,
> The fivefold, equal taste, the four letters,
> Pacification, exorcism, Great Completeness,
> Instructions on the view of the Middle Way School,
>   and so forth,

When these are analyzed by an experienced yogi
Skilled in definitive scripture and reasoning,
They come down to the same thought.

Nevertheless, some Geluk lamas such as the Third Panchen Lama, Losang Belden Yeshe (*blo bzang dpal ldan ye shes,* 1737-1780), have said that the First Panchen Lama had a political purpose in saying so and did not actually hold that the thought of the various schools is basically the same. Their reason for suspecting such is that in Nyingma the view of the Great Completeness is an affirming negative (*paryudāsapratiṣedha, ma yin dgag*), whereas in Geluk it is a non-affirming negative (*prasajyapratiṣedha, med dgag*), due to which they feel that there is no way the two could be getting at the same thing. This point has given rise to many disagreements, with scholars refuting each other and presenting their own positions.

Within Kagyu and Sakya, there are many explicit refutations pertaining to the Great Completeness system, and even though in later Geluk works there are also many, in the writings of Tsongkhapa upon which Geluk is based the terms "Nyingma" or "Great Completeness" are not even mentioned. Those who did take objection were refuting specific points as explained by certain persons, but their style can easily give the unfortunate impression that the Great Completeness is being refuted as a whole—a sad state of affairs.

In my opinion, there is no question that the First Panchen Lama meant that all four schools are getting at the same thing, and it is also undeniable that many practitioners have become highly developed yogis based on the Nyingma Great Completeness teachings. If a yogi can develop fully qualified realization based on a path, then that path is a pure one. Thus, I have given much consideration to how these two presentations could be coming down to the same thing, and although I have formed some ideas on this,

I cannot explain them with complete decision and clarity. More analysis is needed, but let me give you my thought, which is primarily based on the work of the Nyingma master Dodrupchen Jikme Tenpe Nyima (*'jigs med bstan pa'i nyi ma, rdo grub chen III,* 1865-1926), whose writings are the key for my analysis.

What is the frame of reference for the First Panchen Lama's saying that these systems all come down to the same thought? It would be too rough to say that the Middle Way view and the Nyingma Great Completeness have the same thought. For the Middle Way view is held in common even with Hearer Vehicle practitioners[36] according to the explanation of Chandrakīrti's Middle Way Consequence School, whereas the Great Completeness is not found even in the Sūtra Great Vehicle, much less in the Hearer Vehicle. In the Nyingma arrangement of nine vehicles, there are three sūtra vehicles—of Hearers, Solitary Realizers, and Bodhisattvas; three external tantric systems—Kriyā, Upa, and Yoga; and three internal tantric systems—Mahāyoga, Anuyoga, and Atiyoga. Even within the six tantric vehicles, the Great Completeness is not to be found in the three external or even in the Mahāyoga and Anuyoga divisions of the internal; it is the practice of only the peak of vehicles, the great Atiyoga. One could not possibly say that the Great Completeness system, the acme of all these nine vehicles, is the same as the Middle Way system explained by Nāgārjuna. For the Middle Way view is practiced in common even by Hearers and Solitary Realizers who have reached the level of Stream Enterer [that is to say, have directly realized the truth of the emptiness of inherent existence]. Hence, the views of the Great Completeness and Middle Way are not comparable; to compare the Great Completeness with cultivation of the view of the Middle Way School in general is too wide.

Then, if the place of union of this highest of all tantric systems in Nyingma and the view of the New Translation Schools cannot be in terms of the sūtra explanation of the Middle Way School, what is comparable with the view of the Great Completeness? In Highest Yoga Tantras such as the *Guhyasamāja Tantra* as practiced in the New Translation Schools, there is a mode of cultivating the view of the Middle Way School with a special mind, the innate wisdom of great bliss. When its mode of cultivation and that of the Great Completeness in the Old Translation School of Nyingma are seen to be parallel, the comparison is being made at the right level.

In the New Translation Schools' explanation of the *Guhyasamāja Tantra,* the discussion of the view is divided into two parts—objective and subjective views. The objective view refers to the view as object, that is, the emptiness of inherent existence which is the object of the wisdom consciousness, and regarding this the *Guhyasamāja Tantra* does not differ in the least from Nāgārjuna's Middle Way system. However, it differs greatly in terms of the subjective view, the consciousness that is realizing emptiness: According to the Guhyasamāja system, during the completion stage, emptiness is to be realized with an enhanced, more subtle consciousness called the fundamental innate mind of clear light, whereas in the Middle Way School it is realized by a consciousness that, relative to the mind of clear light, is coarse.

According to Tamtsik Dorje (*dam tshig rdo rje*), a Mongolian from Khalkha, when the view of the Great Completeness is taught, it also is divided into two categories, objective and subjective. The former can be understood in the vocabulary of the New Translation Schools, just explained, as the objective clear light, that is to say, as the emptiness that is the object of a wisdom consciousness; the subjective view is a subtle wisdom consciousness, basic mind, not an ordinary coarse consciousness. In the Great Completeness the term "view" most frequently refers not to the object emptiness, but to the subject, the wisdom consciousness and, more or less, a union of the object (emptiness) with the subject (the wisdom consciousness realizing it). This fundamental innate mind of clear light is emphasized equally in the Highest Yoga Tantra systems of the New Translation Schools and in the Nyingma system of the Great Completeness and is the proper place of comparison of the old and new schools.

The treatment of the object, emptiness, as the view and also of the subject, the wisdom consciousness, as the view is not a unique feature of tantra but is similar to the Middle Way Autonomy School's presentation of emptiness as the ultimate truth and the mind realizing emptiness as a concordant ultimate [this being accepted by both the Old and New Translation Schools]. In the Great Completeness, however, the subjective view, that is to say, the mind that takes emptiness as its object—is not the ordinary or coarse mind described in the Perfection Vehicle of the Great Vehicle but a subtle mind. It is basic knowledge (*rig pa*), clear light (*'od gsal*), the fundamental innate mind of clear light (*gnyug ma lhan cig skyes pa'i 'od gsal gyi sems*) which is the final status (*gnas lugs*) of things.

From the viewpoint of the two truths as posited in the Middle Way School, this very subtle mind of clear light would be considered a concordant ultimate and an actual conventionality, not an actual ultimate truth. For in the Middle Way School an actual ultimate truth is an object found by a consciousness distinguishing the final mode of being of objects—emptiness—whereas an object found by a consciousness distinguishing a conventional object [anything except emptiness] is a conventional truth. However, the two truths as they appear in the texts of the Great Completeness are not those of the Middle Way School because they are not based on a distinction between object and subject in the realization of reality but accord with the unique understanding of the two truths in Highest Yoga Tantra.

The Nyingma master Dodrupchen speaks of "special two truths" near the beginning of his *General Meaning of the "Secret Matrix Tantra"* (*gsang ba snying po'i spyi don*).³⁷ He describes seven special ultimate truths—the bases, the path, and the fruit, which is further divided into five categories. The root-principle of this doctrine is the mind-vajra, which is the basis of all the phenomena of cyclic existence and nirvana. In the New Translation Schools' explanations of Highest Yoga Mantra, this is known as the fundamental innate clear light, designated with the name "ultimate truth." In the Great Completeness of Nyingma this fundamental mind or basic knowledge is the ultimate truth, and the appearances of it as impure and pure phenomena are posited as conventional truths. Conventional truths are coarse adventitious phenomena, whereas ultimate truth refers to what is fundamental and innate, the mind-vajra which always exists. This is the unique presentation of the two truths according to the Great Completeness.

Even though the terms—ultimate and conventional—are the same as those used in the Middle Way School, their meaning is different, and we should take care not to confuse them. This difference of meaning is not unprecedented, for even within the Middle Way School, the term "ultimate" is used in different ways. For instance, Maitreya's *Sublime Continuum of the Great Vehicle* speaks of ultimate and conventional refuge, and his *Differentiation of the Middle and the Extremes* (*madhyāntavibhaṅga, dbus mtha' rnam 'byed*) describes the ultimate in three ways. There the objective ultimate is emptiness; the practical ultimate is a wisdom consciousness of meditative equipoise; and the attained ultimate is nirvana.

Also, even the New Translation Schools use the terms "ultimate" and "conventional" in different ways; for example, in their descriptions of the five stages of Highest Yoga Tantra they speak of completion stages of ultimate truth and completion stages of conventional truth with a meaning different from that in their own usage of the terms "ultimate" and "conventional" in the Middle Way School. As in the Great Completeness, this doctrine involves an uncommon understanding of the two truths. The subjective clear light [the very subtle mind of clear light which is the fourth of the five stages in the completion stage] is designated with the name "ultimate truth" in the New Translation Schools; according to the differentiation of the two truths in the Middle Way School, however, this would be a conventional truth, for it would only be a concordant ultimate truth, not an actual one.

Thus, in the Highest Yoga Tantra system of the New Translation Schools, the fundamental mind which serves as the basis of all the phenomena of cyclic existence and nirvana is posited as the ultimate truth or nature of phenomena (*dharmatā, chos nyid*); it is also sometimes called the "clear light" (*ābhāsvara, 'od gsal*) and "uncompounded" (*asaṃskṛta, 'dus ma byas*). In Nyingma it is called the "mind-vajra"; this is not the mind that is contrasted with basic knowledge in the division into basic knowledge (*rig pa*) and mind (*sems*) but the factor of mere luminosity and knowing, basic knowledge itself. This is the final root of all minds, forever indestructible, immutable, and of unbreakable continuum like a vajra [or diamond]. Just as the New Translation Schools posit a beginningless and endless fundamental mind, so Nyingma posits a mind-vajra which has no beginning or end and proceeds without interruption through the effect stage of Buddhahood. It is considered "permanent" in the sense of abiding forever and thus is presented as a permanent mind. It is permanent not in the sense of not disintegrating moment by moment but in the sense that its continuum is not interrupted—this being analogous to the statement in Maitreya's *Ornament for Clear Realization* that a Buddha's exalted activities are considered permanent in that they are inexhaustible. It is also non-produced in the sense that it is not adventitiously and newly produced by causes and conditions [since its continuum has always existed].

In the same vein, the Geluk scholar and adept Norsang Gyatso (*nor bzang rgya mtsho,* 1423–1513) says that whatever exists is necessarily compounded (*saṃskṛta, 'dus byas*), though his referent is more general than the usual meaning of "compounded." He is not asserting that all phenomena, including permanent phenomena, are produced upon the aggregation of causes and conditions but that all phenomena exist conditionally, in dependence both on their parts and on a conceptual consciousness that designates them. Similarly, because this basic mind of Nyingma is not newly produced in dependence upon causes and conditions, it is called "non-produced," the reference being to a broader sense of the term.

In Nyingma, the mind-vajra is posited as the ultimate truth. This ultimate truth is not posited from the viewpoint of being an object found by a consciousness distinguishing emptiness as in the Middle Way School; rather, it is the fundamental mind of clear light which has no beginning and no end, the basis of all the phenomena of cyclic existence and of nirvana. It has a nature of the Truth Body of the effect stage of Buddhahood. Being beyond all adventitious phenomena, it is called the ultimate truth. The sport, manifestations, or coarse forms of it are conventional truths.

The entity (*ngo bo*) of this basic mind is essentially pure (*ka dag*) or, in the vocabulary of the Middle Way School, naturally devoid of inherent existence from the very start. Within the sphere of this nature of mere luminosity and knowing, all pure and impure phenomena appear as the sport, or manifestation, of its spontaneous nature. All such appearing and occurring phenomena are characterized by this nature (*rang bzhin*) of spontaneity (*lhun grub*). The unimpeded effulgence of the basic mind is called "compassion" (*thugs rje*) because its effect is the compassionate activities of a

Buddha, which are based on the essentially pure entity and spontaneous nature of the mind-vajra.

Naturally pure from the start and endowed with a spontaneous nature, the mind-vajra is the basis of all the phenomena occurring in cyclic existence and nirvana. Even while one is still a sentient being and despite the generation of a great many good and bad conceptions such as manifest desire, hatred, and bewilderment, the mind-vajra itself is free from the pollutions of these defilements. Water may be extremely dirty; yet its nature remains just clear—its nature is not polluted by dirt. Similarly, no matter what afflictive emotions are generated as the sport of this mind-vajra and no matter how powerful they are, the basic mind itself, the basis of the appearance of such artifice, remains unaffected by defilement, beginninglessly good, all-good (*samantabhadra, kun tu bzang po*).

The exalted qualities of the effect stage of Buddhahood, such as the ten powers and the four fearlessnesses, are all present in substance in this mind-vajra; their manifestation is prevented only by the presence of certain conditions. Thus, it is said that we are enlightened from the very beginning, endowed with a completely good basic mind.

If one identifies this suchness, ultimate truth, or basic mind and ascertains that all phenomena of cyclic existence and nirvana are its sport, then along the way one understands that all pure and impure phenomena are, as the texts of the Middle Way School say, only nominally existent. One understands that all appearing and occurring objects of knowledge are adventitious and essenceless, that although such phenomena have from the start not been established under their own power, they nonetheless appear to us to have their own autonomous nature, whereupon we adhere to this sense of seeming inherent existence. One further understands that this misapprehension leads to engagement in various good and bad actions and accumulation of those predispositions, leading to still more entanglement in cyclic existence. However, if one can cause all these phenomena to appear as the sport of basic mind within not deviating from the sphere of that mind, one does not come under the influence of conventional conceptions. When we identify our own basic entity ourselves and directly ascertain its meaning continuously and forever in meditative equipoise, then even though acting in the world, we are Buddhas.

In a similar way, in the New Translation Schools, it is said that when the clear light is actualized, the great yogi rests. In the vocabulary of the New Translation Schools, all the conceptual elaborations causing actions that result in the accumulation of predispositions are consciousnesses more coarse than even the minds of appearance, increase, and near-attainment[38] which must cease before the mind of clear light can dawn. Having manifested the mind of clear light, if we are unable to remain in it, the minds of near-attainment, increase, and appearance will be generated, and the eighty conceptions[39] will arise, from which contaminated actions will once again occur, and their predispositions will accumulate. This is what causes harm. However, when the eighty conceptions as well as the three minds of appearance, increase, and near-attainment cease and we steadily abide in the clear light, afflictive emotions and conceptions cannot be generated. Remaining within this state, we are beyond the scope of conceptuality; not even the strongest of afflictive emotions can intrude at this stage. It is a real rest.

That is the presentation of the New Translation Schools. In Nyingma vocabulary, if one comes to understand the reality of the mind-vajra, this mode of subsistence, one understands all appearances of cyclic existence and nirvana as arising through its force, as its sport, through which one realizes that these phenomena do not exist in their own right but through the force of this basic mind. Just as in Nāgārjuna's *Precious Garland*[40] cyclic existence is shown to be false because it arises in dependence on a false cause—ignorance, so though the basic mind is not itself false, the phenomena of cyclic existence and nirvana are the sport of the basic mind, yet do not appear as such, and from this point of view are shown to be false. Through realizing this, one perforce understands that these phenomena exist only nominally. Dodrupchen says that when we are able to ascertain all appearing and occurring objects of knowledge as the sport of the basic mind, we perforce understand even better the position of the Consequence School that these exist only through the power of conceptuality.

The Great Completeness presents a practice of viewing all phenomena of cyclic existence and nirvana as the sport and the self-effulgence of the mind within sustaining awareness of the basic entity of the mind. Even though there is little explanation of the elimination of the object of negation, inherent existence, and of the realization of phenomena as nominally designated, such is understood as a by-product right along with understanding that all of these phenomena are just the manifestations, or sport, of this basic mind of clear light. Therefore, all the important points of the view of emptiness as found in the New Translation Schools' presentation of the Middle Way School are contained within this practice.

In the Middle Way Consequence School, this realization is described in terms of understanding that phenomena exist only through the force of nominal conventions and not inherently. According to Geluk and other explanations, during meditation only the absence of inherent existence is taken as the object of one's mode of apprehension, not anything else—just the mere negative of the inherent existence which is the object of negation. The practitioner seeks to remain in meditation without losing that object. A consciousness ascertaining this meaning must have the aspect of realizing a non-affirming negative, a negation that does not imply anything positive in its place. It is a fundamental tenet of the Middle Way system that emptiness is a non-affirming negative. Bhāvaviveka, for instance, explains this point clearly in his commentary on the first stanza of the first chapter of Nāgārjuna's *Treatise on the Middle* where Nāgārjuna says that things are not produced from self, other, both, or causelessly. Buddhapālita and Chandrakīrti also say the same.

In the Great Completeness, however, one meditates on the basic mind of clear light, one-pointedly observing the factor of mere luminosity and knowing; thus, this meditative mind does not have the aspect of realizing a mere non-affirming negative. Still, prior to this stage when being introduced to the basic mind in the practice called "breakthrough," the practitioner of the Great Completeness analyzes from where the mind arises, where it abides, and where it goes. In the course of this practice, as in the texts of the Middle Way School, it is ascertained that the mind is devoid of the extremes of conceptual elaboration; this is realization of its absence of inherent existence. Later, in meditating on the basic mind, or clear light, which is free from arising, abiding, and going away, the practitioner is meditating on an affirming negative, in which the basic mind appears but is understood as empty of inherent existence.

In the Nyingma breakthrough system, emptiness is mainly explained in relation to the mind, whereas in the Middle Way system, it is mainly with respect to the person, within a division of all phenomena into persons—or users of objects—and those objects that are used. The practice of emptiness in the breakthrough system is associated with the mind because of the great emphasis in Nyingma on the mind itself, cognition, the basic mind. Āryadeva in his *Lamp Compendium for Practice,* a commentary on the five stages of the *Guhyasamāja Tantra* which is a principal Highest Yoga Tantra of the New Translation Schools and especially of Geluk, says in discussing the third of the five stages, called "mental isolation," that if you do not know the nature of the mind, you cannot be released. He does not say that if you do not know the nature of the person or of an external sprout, you cannot be released. Indeed, there is no difference between the emptiness of the mind and the emptiness of the person or of a sprout in terms of merely being the elimination of inherent existence, but because he is explaining tantra and within that the stage of mental isolation in Highest Yoga Tantra, he emphasizes the difference that comes by way of the consciousness realizing emptiness. Just as Āryadeva stresses the nature of the mind, so does the breakthrough practice of Nyingma, in which one meditates on the mind within understanding it as qualified by an absence of inherent existence.

In Nyingma there is no clear and detailed explanation of whether this combination of mind and emptiness is an affirming negative or a non-affirming negative; however, a few Nyingma scholars have said that it is the former. Due to this, some people say that there is no way those who assert that the view is a non-affirming negative could agree with those who assert that the view is an affirming negative. However, the issue is more complex than that.

Even in the sūtra explanation of meditation, there are two basic types—(1) meditation on an objective aspect as in meditating on impermanence and (2) meditation, or generation, of the subject into a different type of subject as in the case of cultivating love. When in Nyingma we "meditate" on the profound mind, the mind itself is identifying the profound nature of the mind and sustaining it in meditation in the style of the second type of meditation. When this profound mind identifies itself, just it is manifest. Since, prior to contacting and identifying the entity of this profound mind, one has already ascertained the emptiness of inherent existence of the mind through the practice of breakthrough by watching from what the mind arises, where it abides, and into what it goes, a mind that is understood as qualified by an emptiness of inherent existence appears. Even though this can be termed meditation on an affirming negative, this is not like the affirming negative of illusory-like appearance—a composite of appearance and emptiness—which is meditated with a coarser level of consciousness in the Middle Way School. Rather, the meditation itself proceeds with a subtler mind. As familiarity with the basic mind grows stronger, the complex of conceptions gradually decreases, consciousness becomes more and more subtle, and the clear light is manifested.

Even in the New Translation Schools, when the clear light is manifested, the emptiness of inherent existence appears. According to the explanation of the Geluk scholar and adept Norsang Gyatso, when the mother clear light[41] appears even to an ordinary person at death, emptiness appears but is not ascertained. For when any being, even a bug, dies, there is a vanishing of coarse dualistic appearance; it is not that the appearance of inherent existence or conventional appearances vanish but that coarser conventional appearances do. Thus, it is said that at the time of the clear light of death emptiness appears but that the person, unless a highly developed yogi, cannot ascertain it because it is not appearing due to the elimination of the object of negation, inherent existence. However, when the mind identifies itself, and this is done by a person who has ascertained emptiness, then when for that person dualistic appearance vanishes, there is no doubt that this mind is one undifferentiable entity with emptiness and that a vanishing of dualistic appearance into emptiness is being fully realized.

In the Great Completeness, as a yogi grows more and more

accustomed to meditating on the composite of emptiness and appearance with respect to a subtle mind—the appearance yet emptiness of this basic mind, the mind being understood as qualified by an emptiness of inherent existence—the appearance of conceptual elaborations gradually diminishes in the sphere of the basic mind, allowing the very subtle clear light to manifest. It is thus apparent that all the factors involved in cultivating the view of emptiness as presented in texts common to sūtra and mantra in the New Translation Schools are contained in Great Completeness meditation.

That is the way the ultimate truth, the basic mind, is meditated in the Great Completeness doctrine of Nyingma. In the New Translation Schools, actualization of the fundamental mind simultaneous with the manifestation of the six operative consciousnesses [eye, ear, nose, tongue, body, and mental consciousnesses] is impossible. It is necessary first to dissolve all coarser consciousnesses, to render them as though incapacitated; only then will the fundamental mind nakedly appear. It is impossible for coarse and subtle consciousnesses—functioning to comprehend objects—to occur simultaneously.

However, in the Old Translation School of the Great Completeness, it is possible to be introduced to the clear light without the cessation of the six operative consciousnesses. Even when an afflictive emotion is generated in an encounter with an object upon which we falsely superimpose a goodness or badness beyond its actual nature, the afflictive emotion itself has the nature of being an entity of mere luminosity and knowing. Since the mind of clear light has the general character of mind as an entity of mere luminosity and knowing, the general factor of the clear light can be identified even in the midst of a coarse afflictive consciousness such as desire or hatred. As Dodrupchen says, the factor of mere luminosity and knowing pervades all consciousnesses and can even be identified during the generation of a strong afflictive emotion without having to cease the six operative consciousnesses.

In a similar way, the *Kālachakra Tantra* speaks of the possibility of generating an empty form,[42] an appearance of the fundamental mind, without actualizing the fundamental mind itself. It is said that a child who knows nothing of Buddhist tenets can succeed at making an empty form just in play. Whereas an empty form is necessarily an appearance of the subtle basic mind, it is not necessary to stop the six operative consciousnesses and manifest this subtlest mind in order for such an appearance to occur. This is similar to the Great Completeness doctrine in which, to identify the factor of mere luminosity and knowing, it is not necessary to cease the six consciousnesses and manifest the subtlest mind of clear light. Still, when a yogi practicing either the Great Completeness or the *Kālachakra Tantra* attains a high level of proficiency, the six operative consciousnesses stop and the subtlest mind manifests as in the Secret Mantra path of the New Translation Schools. The difference is that when beginning the practice of identifying the basic mind in the Great Completeness, such stoppage of the six operative consciousnesses is not necessary. Rather, leaving the coarser consciousnesses as they are, the yogi identifies the clear light.

When this has been done, it is not necessary purposely to eliminate conceptions of goodness and badness. Instead, no matter what type of conception may arise, it has no power of deception over the practitioner, who is able to remain focused one-pointedly on the factor of mere luminosity and knowing. Thereby, the conditions for generating the improper mental application of making false superimpositions upon phenomena diminish in strength, and conceptuality cannot really get started, gradually lessening in strength. In this way the doctrine of the Great Completeness comes to have a unique mode of presenting the view, meditation, and behavior for someone who has been introduced to the basic mind and has identified it well.

Hence, there are modes of practice of the fundamental mind according to (1) the explanation of the *Guhyasamāja Tantra* by the New Translation Schools, (2) the Kālachakra doctrine of empty form and so forth, and (3) the Great Completeness doctrine of Nyingma. According to the New Translation Schools, at a certain high point in the practice of Secret Mantra, the māntrika engages in special practices such as making use of a sexual partner, hunting animals, and so forth. Though it is easy to explain the purpose of employing a partner as a means of bringing desire to the path and inducing subtler consciousnesses realizing emptiness, the hunting of animals cannot be explained that way. Its uncommon purpose is limited to those who have brought familiarity with the fundamental mind to such a high level that they have great confidence in its practice; these practitioners have passed beyond the scope of conceptuality. For those with such a nature, no conception is one-pointedly good or bad; it is within this high situation that anger is utilized in the path with a compassionate motivation. Thus, the basis of this practice in the New Translation Schools is the same as that of the Great Completeness.

This important unifying doctrine is illuminated through bringing together the explanations of the view in the Middle Way School, *Guhyasamāja, Kālachakra,* Mother Tantras such as *Chakrasaṃvara,* the Great Completeness, and Do-drup-chen's key-like explanation. However, it is also essential to meet and consult with an experienced lama. The foundation for my explanation derives from the teachings of the fully qualified Nyingma scholar and adept Dodrupchen Jikme Tenpe Nyima. This very special being was the student of Jamyang Khyentse Wangpo (*'jam dbyangs mkhyen brtse dbang po,* 1820–1892), who himself was an incarnation of the King Trisong Detsen, as well as an amazing lama free from bias concerning the views of Nyingma, Sakya, Kagyu, and Geluk. In his late teens Dodrupchen was already skilled in many texts of the Middle Way, the Perfection of Wisdom, Valid Cognition, and the New Translation Schools' explanations of the *Kālachakra Tantra* and the *Guhyasamāja Tantra*, as well as the Great Completeness, his own unique specialty.

I had earlier noticed in Tsongkhapa's explanation of the hidden meaning of the first forty syllables in the introduction to the *Guhyasamāja Tantra* a quote from Nāgārjuna's *Five Stages* (*pañca-krama, rim pa lnga*): "Everything is like the meditative stabilization of illusion." In quoting this, Tsongkhapa establishes that all environments and beings are the sport of mere wind and mind. Finding there the scent of a profound doctrine, I took his statement as a basis and explored these several corresponding teachings. Reading Dodrupchen was as if he were stroking my head in confirmation, giving me confidence that my insight was not unfounded. However, I cannot claim definite knowledge; it is just my estimation of how it must be. One needs to become skilled in the Middle Way School, the *Guhyasamāja Tantra,* and the *Kālachakra Tantra* and look into Dodrupchen's *General Meaning of the "Secret Matrix Tantra."*

It is clear that the reasoning of the Epistemologists (*prāmāṇika, tshad ma pa*)[43] and Proponents of the Middle Way is not sufficient to explain the mode of procedure of high levels of practice in Secret Mantra, whether in the Old or New Translation Schools. For instance, in the Guhyasamāja system certain forms are posited as paths,[44] and the exalted wisdom of the actual clear light of the fourth stage [in the completion stage] can instantaneously act as an antidote to both the artificial and innate afflictive obstructions.[45] Such points cannot be explained without knowledge of the subtler winds and the consciousnesses mounted upon them as described in Highest Yoga Tantra; the procedures of the Episte-mologists and Proponents of the Middle Way alone are not sufficient. Similarly, even within the New Translation Schools it is difficult for someone who has only studied the Guhyasamāja sys-tem to believe the structure of channels and winds as set forth in the Kālachakra system or the mode of establishing, in dependence on them, an empty form that serves as a cause generating the supreme immutable bliss whereupon the twenty-one thousand six hundred material factors in the body are consumed by the twenty-one thousand six hundred white and red essential drops, causing the twenty-one thousand six hundred latencies of emission to be overcome, resulting in actualization of Buddhahood. Only in dependence on a qualified and experienced lama's decisive expla-nation that such is a valid path set forth in certain tantras and that through it certain realizations are generated can persons who have confined their study to another system come to accept this.

In a similar way, the Great Completeness way of presenting the paths and so forth as, for instance, in Longchenpa's (klong chen pa dri med 'od zer, 1308-1363) Treasury of the Supreme Vehicle (theg pa'i mchog rin po che'i mdzod), differs in small ways from those presented in the New Translation Schools. Since these presentations were taught for persons of various types and since all are based on the general Buddhist foundation of the two truths, their differences are only uncommon distinctive features. Thus, a particular pres-entation cannot be faulted merely for disagreeing with the pres-entation to which one is accustomed.

In the same way, due to differences in yogis' bodies, the struc-ture of the channels and the order of the appearances that occur in dependence upon them are explained differently in the Guhyasamāja, Kālachakra, and Great Completeness systems. For instance, in Guhyasamāja there are thirty-two channel petals or spokes at the crown of the head and sixteen at the throat, whereas it is the opposite in Kālachakra. Also, in the stages of dissolution, mirage appears before smoke in Guhyasamāja, whereas it is the other way around in Kālachakra, with the former system having a total of eight signs but the latter having ten. There are similar differences with the Great Completeness system.

The various systems present what are merely different techniques for manifesting the fundamental mind of clear light. In the Guhyasamāja system there is yoga of the inner winds [currents of energy]. In the Chakrasaṃvara system there is generation of the four blisses. The Hevajra system emphasizes the inner heat, called the "fierce woman" (caṇḍālī, gtum mo). Kālachakra involves the practice of concentrating on empty form. A distinctive feature of the Great Completeness is that a yogi can induce appearance of the fundamental mind of clear light, not through engaging in reasoning and so forth, but just through sustaining a state of non-conceptuality in combination with various external and internal conditions. There is also a similar practice in the Kagyu system of the Great Seal (mahāmudrā, phyag rgya chen po).

With respect to identifying the clear light in the Great Completeness: When, for instance, one hears a noise, between the time of hearing it and conceptualizing it as such and such, there is a type of mind devoid of conceptuality but nevertheless not like sleep or meditative stabilization, in which the object is a reflection of this entity of mere luminosity and knowing. It is at such a point that the basic entity of the mind is identified. Those training in philosophy in the New Translation Schools who frequently repeat the definition of consciousness, "that which is luminous and knowing," need to identify it in experience. It is not sufficient merely to mouth definitions, divisions, and illustrations; experience is necessary, and for this the Great Completeness is extremely valuable. It introduces one to the actuality of this entity of mere luminosity and knowing.

It is said in the Great Completeness teachings that one cannot become enlightened through a fabricated mind; rather, basic mind is to be identified, whereupon all phenomena are to be understood as the sport of that mind, continuous ascertainment being induced one-pointedly with respect to this. With such practice it is not necessary to repeat mantra, recite texts, and so forth because one has something greater. These other practices are fabricated; they require exertion whereas when one identifies the basic mind and sustains practice within this, it is a spontaneous practice without exertion. Practices requiring exertion are done by the mind, but spontaneous practices without exertion are done by basic mind.

To do this, it is not sufficient merely to read books; one needs the full preparatory practice of the Nyingma system and, in addition, needs the special teaching of a qualified Nyingma master as well as his or her blessings. Still, the student must also have accumulated great merit. The great Jikme Lingpa (*'jigs med gling pa*, 1729/30-1798) himself spent three years and three phases of the moon[46] in retreat with tremendous effort after which the sphere of the basic mind manifested; it did not come easily. Dodrupchen similarly worked very hard; throughout his writings he emphasizes that someone engaging in this spontaneous practice without exertion must work hard at all the preparatory practices, be introduced to basic mind by a lama with actual experience, and meditate on it one-pointedly within total renunciation of this life. He says that through this the sphere of basic mind can be identified, not otherwise.

Some people, however, mistake the doctrine about the non-necessity of repeating mantra, meditating on a deity, and so forth and think that the Great Completeness is easy. Such is really foolish. It is not easy at all. Someone who does not know the view of the Middle Way School and does not have experience with the altruistic intention to become enlightened would probably find it impossible. With such background, however, great progress can be made.

As the result of such complete practice, we achieve a union of the Truth and Form Bodies of a Buddha. According to the Guhyasamāja system, this is achieved in dependence upon the practice of the union of the conventional illusory body and the ultimate clear light. In the Kālachakra system the same is achieved in dependence upon the union of empty form and immutable bliss. In the Great Completeness it is achieved through the unification of view and meditation, or breakthrough and leap-over.[47] The substance of all of these paths comes down to the fundamental innate mind of clear light. Even the sūtras serving as the basis for Maitreya's exposition in his *Sublime Continuum of the Great Vehicle* have this same fundamental mind as the basis of their thought in their discussion of the Buddha nature, or matrix-of-One-Gone-Thus, although the full mode of its practice is not described as it is in the systems of Highest Yoga Tantra.

This is the point of comparison where these various systems come together. Transcending sectarianism, we can find much to evoke deep realization by seeing how these schools come down to the same basic thought.

NOTES

...

1 The location of the main venue for each chapter is given after the chapter title; often, teachings from multiple locations are edited into a single chapter.

2 For more on cultivation of the seven cause and effect quintessential instructions, see His Holiness the Dalai Lama, *How to Expand Love: Widening the Circle of Loving Relationships,* trans. and ed. by Jeffrey Hopkins (New York: Atria, 2005).

3 XXVII.30: *gang gis thugs brtse nyer bzung nas// lta ba thams cad spang ba'i phyir// dam pa'i chos ni bstan mdzad pa// gau tam de la phyag 'tshal lo//;* Sanskrit: *sarvadṛṣṭiprahāṇāya yaḥ saddharmamadeśayat/ anukampāmapādāya taṃ namasyāmi gautamaṃ;* both as found in Louis de La Vallée Poussin, *Mūlamadhyamakakārikās de Nāgārjuna avec la Prasannapadā commentaire de Candrakīrti,* Bibliotheca Buddhica 4 (Osnabrück, Germany: Biblio Verlag, 1970), 592.

4 The *Vajrapañjara Tantra* says:

> Action Tantras are for the inferior.
> Yoga without actions is for those above them.
> The supreme Yoga is for supreme beings.
> The Highest Yoga is for those above them.

See H.H. the Dalai Lama, Tsong-ka-pa, and Jeffrey Hopkins, *Tantra in Tibet* (London: George Allen and Unwin, 1977; reprint, with minor corrections, Ithaca, N.Y.: Snow Lion Publications, 1987), 151.

5 For a complete translation of this text, see Tsong-kha-pa, *The Great Treatise on the Stages of the Path to Enlightenment,* vols. 1–3, ed. Joshua W. C. Cutler and Guy Newland (Ithaca, N.Y.: Snow Lion Publications, 2000–2003).

6 The translation of Tsongkhapa's text is taken, with slight modification, from Geshe Lhundup Sopa and Jeffrey Hopkins, *Cutting through Appearances: The Practice and Theory of Tibetan Buddhism* (Ithaca, N.Y.: Snow Lion Publications, 1989).

7 *khyod kyis ji snyed bka' stsal pa// rten 'brel nyid las brtsams te 'jug/ de yang mya ngan 'da' phyir te// zhi 'gyur min mdzad khyod la med//;* P6016, vol. 153, 38.1.1–38.1.3.

8 XII.13: *zhi sgo gnyis pa med pa dang//;* (Varanasi: Pleasure of Elegant Sayings, 1974), 140.7. Sanskrit: *advitīyaṃ śivadvāraṃ,* in Karen Lang, *Āryadeva's Catuḥśataka: On the Bodhisattva's Cultivation of Merit and Knowledge.* Indiske Studier 7 (Copenhagen: Akademisk Forlag, 1986), 114. This passage is treated in Chandrakīrti's *Commentary on (Āryadeva's) "Four Hundred"* (*Bodhisattva-yogācāracatuḥśatakaṭīkā, byang chub sems dpa'i rnal 'byor spyod pa bzhi brgya pa'i rgya cher 'grel pa*), *sDe dge Tibetan Tripiṭaka—bsTan hgyur preserved at the Faculty of Letters, University of Tokyo* (Tokyo, 1979), vol. 8 (No.3865), 190b.1–191a.6. It is discussed in Gyeltsap's *Explanation of (Chandrakīrti's) "Four Hundred," Essence of Eloquence* (*bzhi brgya pa'i rnam bshad legs bshad snying po*) (Sarnath: Pleasure of Elegant Sayings Printing Press, 1971), 9.

9 For a description of the levels of the completion stage, see Daniel Cozort, *Highest Yoga Tantra* (Ithaca, N.Y.: Snow Lion Publications, 1986).

10 The *Four Hundred,* VIII.12: *gang la 'dir skyo yod min pa// de la zhi gus ga la yod//* (Varanasi: Pleasure of Elegant Sayings, 1974), 122.2. Sanskrit: *udvego yasya nāstīha bhaktis tasya kutaḥ śive,* in Lang, *Āryadeva's Catuḥśataka: On the Bodhisattva's Cultivation of Merit and Knowledge,* 82.

11 Dharmakīrti's *Commentary on (Dignāga's) "Compilation of Prime Cognition,"* Chapter II: *sdug bsngal 'khor ba can phung po//* (Varanasi: Pleasure of Elegant Sayings, 1974), 56.7. Sanskrit: *duḥkhaṃ saṃsāriṇaḥ skandhāḥ,* as found in Swami Dwarikadas Shastri, *Pramāṇavārttika of Āchārya Dharmakīrtti* (Varanasi: Bauddha Bharati, 1968), 54.8.

12 V.1: *srid pa'i rtsa ba phra rgyas drug* (Varanasi: Pleasure of Elegant Sayings, 1978), 205.2.

13 Dharmakīrti's *Commentary on (Dignāga's) "Compilation of Prime Cognition,"* Chapter II: *sems kyi rang bzhin 'od gsal te// dri ma rnams ni blo bur ba//* (Varanasi: Pleasure of Elegant Sayings, 1974), 63.11. Sanskrit: *prabhāsvaramidaṃ cittaṃ prakṛtyāgantatro malāḥ,* as found in Shastri, *Pramāṇavārttika of Āchārya Dharmakīrtti,* 73.1.

14 *Engaging in the Bodhisattva Deeds,* V.109cd: *sman dpyad bklags pa tsam gyis ni// nad pa dag la phan 'gyur ram//;* Sanskrit: *cikitsāpāṭhamātreṇa rogiṇaḥ kiṃ bhaviṣyati;* both as found in *Bodhicaryāvatāra,* ed. by Vidhushekhara

Bhattacharya, Bibliotheca Indica vol. 280 (Calcutta: The Asiatic Society, 1960), 79–80.

15 *Engaging in the Bodhisattva Deeds,* VI.14ab: *goms na sla bar mi 'gyur ba'i // dngos de gang yang yod ma yin//*; Sanskrit: *na kiṃcidasti tadvastu yadabhyāsasya duṣkaram*; both as found in *Bodhicaryāvatāra,* ed. by Vidhushekhara Bhattacharya, 83.

16 I.28: *sdug bsngal 'dor 'dod sems yod kyang// sdug bsngal nyid la mngon par rgyug// bde ba 'dod kyang gti mug pas// rang gi bde ba dgra ltar 'joms//*; Sanskrit: *duḥkhamevābhidhāvanti duḥkhaniḥśaraṇāśayā// sukhecchayaiva saṃmohāt svasukhaṃ ghnanti śatruvat*; both as found in *Bodhicaryāvatāra,* ed. by Vidhushekhara Bhattacharya, 9.

17 Chapter II: *brtse ldan sdug bsngal gzhom pa'i phyir// thabs rnams la ni mngon sbyor mdzad// thabs byung de rgyu lkog gyur pa// de 'chad pa ni dka' ba yin//* (Varanasi: Pleasure of Elegant Sayings, 1974), 54.14. Sanskrit: *dayāvān duḥkhahānārthamupāyeṣvabhiyujyate/ parokṣopeyataddhetostadākhyānaṃ hi duṣkaram,* as found in Shastri, *Pramāṇavārttika of Āchārya Dharmakīrtti,* 50.3.

18 This is an analysis of whether the person and the mind-body complex are inherently the same entity or different entities, whether the person inherently depends on mind and body, whether mind and body inherently depend on the person, whether the person inherently possesses mind and body, whether the person is the shape of the body, and whether the person is the composite of mind and body. See Jeffrey Hopkins, *Meditation on Emptiness* (London: Wisdom Publications, 1983; rev. ed., Boston: Wisdom Publications, 1996), Part One, Chapters 3 & 4; Part Two, Chapter 5; and Part Six, Chapter 7.

19 XXIV.19: *gang phyir rten 'byung ma yin pa'i // chos 'ga' yod pa ma yin pa// de phyir stong pa ma yin pa'i // chos 'ga' yod pa ma yin no//*; Sanskrit: *apratītya samutpanno dharmaḥ kaścinna vidyate/ yasmāttasmādaśūnyo 'hi dharmaḥ kaścinna vidyate*; both as found in Louis de La Vallée Poussin, *Madhyamakāvatāra par Candrakīrti,* Bibliotheca Buddhica 9 (Osnabrück: Biblio Verlag, 1970), 505.

20 XIV.23; P5246, Vol.95 139.2.7. *'di kun rang dbang med pa ste// des na bdag ni yod ma yin//,* as found in La Vallée Poussin, *Madhyamakāvatāra par Candrakīrti,* 279; no extant Sanskrit. Bracketed additions are from Chandrakīrti's commentary (P5266, vol.98, 270.3.6).

21 VI.160: *rnam bdun gyis med gang de ji lta bur// yod ces rnal 'byor pas 'di'i yod mi rnyed// des de nyid la'ang bde blag 'jug 'gyur bas// 'dir de'i grub pa*

de bzhin 'dod par bya//. The bracketed material is from Tsongkhapa's *Illumination of the Thought (dgongs pa rab gsal)* (Dharamsala: Shes rig par khang edition, n.d.), 218.14-218.19.

22 See his four volumes of *Cases of the Reincarnation Type* published by the University Press of Virginia, Charlottesville.

23 See His Holiness the Dalai Lama, *Mind of Clear Light: How to Live Well and Die Consciously* (formerly, *Advice on Dying*), trans. and ed. by Jeffrey Hopkins (New York: Atria Books/Simon and Schuster, 2002), 136-137; and Lati Rinbochay and Jeffrey Hopkins, *Death, Intermediate State, and Rebirth in Tibetan Buddhism* (London: Rider, 1980; reprint, Ithaca, N.Y.: Snow Lion Publications, 1985), 38-41.

24 For a detailed description of these practices in Action and Performance Tantras, see H.H. the Dalai Lama, Tsong-ka-pa, and Jeffrey Hopkins, *The Yoga of Tibet* (London: George Allen and Unwin, 1981; reprinted as *Deity Yoga*. Ithaca, N.Y.: Snow Lion Publications, 1987).

25 For a detailed description of these practices in Yoga Tantra, see H.H. the Dalai Lama, Dzong-ka-pa, and Jeffrey Hopkins, *Yoga Tantra: Paths to Magical Feats* (Ithaca, N.Y.: Snow Lion Publications, 2005).

26 For a thorough discussion of types of reasons, see Katherine M. Rogers, *Tibetan Logic* (Ithaca, N.Y.: Snow Lion Publications, 2006).

27 For more discussion of a bliss consciousness realizing emptiness, see His Holiness the Dalai Lama, *How to Practice: The Way to a Meaningful Life,* trans. and ed. by Jeffrey Hopkins (New York: Atria, 2002), 192-197.

28 Dates are taken from David L. Snellgrove and Hugh Richardson, *Cultural History of Tibet* (New York: Praeger, 1968) or E. Gene Smith's entries in the Library of Congress card catalogue.

29 P3080, vol. 68 275.3.1. Sahajavajra's commentary is the *Tattvadaśakaṭīkā (de kho na nyid bcu pa'i rgya cher 'grel pa)*, P3099, vol. 68, 297.4.6ff. Mention of "Nāgārjuna, Āryadeva, Chandrakīrti, and so forth" is at 299.1.6 and specific identification of quintessential instructions at 299.2.2, 299.5.3, 300.1.2, and 300.2.3. This passage is quoted and the same remarks are made in Jangkya Rölpe Dorje's *(lcang skya rol pa'i rdo rje,* born 1717) *Presentations of Tenets (grub mtha'i rnam bzhag)* (Sarnath: Pleasure of Elegant Sayings Press, 1970), 297.20.

30 This is a song to five non-human temptresses. For the Tibetan, see *The Complete Biography of Milarepa (rje btsun mi la ras pa'i rnam thar rgyas par phye pa mgur 'bum)* (n.p., 1971), 347.15-8.11. For Garma C.C. Chang's English translation, see *The Hundred Thousand Songs of Milarepa* (Hyde

Park: University Books, 1962), 325. For other songs, see Lama Kunga
Rinpoche and Brian Cutillo, *Drinking the Mountain Stream: Songs of
Tibet's Beloved Saint, Milarepa: Eighteen selections from the rare collection* Sto-
ries and Songs from the Oral Tradition of Jetsün Milarepa (Boston: Wisdom Publications, 1995).

31 For a short biography of Hlodrak Khenchen Namkha Gyeltsen (*lho brag
mkhan chen nam mkha' rgyal mtshan*), see *Lives of the Teachers of the Lam-
rim Precepts* (also called *Biographies of eminent gurus in the transmission lineages of the teachings of the Graduated Path*) (*byang chub lam gyi rim pa'i
rgyan mchog phul byung nor bu'i phreng ba*) by Tsechokling Yongdzin
Yeshe Gyeltsen (*tshe mchog gling yongs 'dzin ye shes rgyal mtshan,* 1713–
1793) (New Delhi: Ngawang Gelek Demo, 1970–1972), 640.5–9.2,
with further mention at 731.6ff. The teaching that Tsongkhapa
received from Namkha Gyeltsen in a visionary meeting with Vajrapāṇi
has been translated by Robert Thurman in *Life and Teachings of Tsong
Khapa* (Dharamsala: Library of Tibetan Works and Archives, 1982), 213–
230. His collected works have been published in two volumes as *Collected Writings of Lho-brag Grub-chen Nam-mkha'-rgyal-mtshan* (New
Delhi: Tshering Dargye, 1972). Namkha Gyeltsen is sometimes placed
as a Kadampa (*bka' gdams pa*), but there is an oral transmission that he
is Nyingma, and it is clear that the teachings on the view that Tsongkhapa received from him are in the unique vocabulary of the Great
Completeness System of Nyingma.

32 *mkhas grub dge legs dpal bzang po'i gsung thor bu'i gras rnams phyogs gcig tu
bsdebs pa, The Collected Works of the Lord Mkhas-grub rJe dGe-legs-dpal-
bzaṅ-po* (New Delhi: Guru Deva, 1980), 125.1–125.6.3.

33 *sbyor sgrol;* rituals involving sexual union and violence.

34 *rma snyegs;* these are Ma Rinchen Chok (*rma rin chen mchog*) and likely
Nyak Jñānakumāra (*gnyags ye shes gzhon nu*), who translated with Ma
Rinchen Chok works such as Vimalamitra's *gsang ba snying po'i 'grel
chung piṇḍārtha.* Thanks to Steven Weinberger and Phillip Stanley for the
identifications.

35 2b.2. The First Panchen Lama, Losang Chökyi Gyeltsen (*blo bzang chos
kyi rgyal mtshan,* 1567[?]–1662), gives brief descriptions of these systems
in his commentary *Extensive Explanation of the Root Text of the Great Seal
in the Traditions of the Precious Geluk Kagyu: Intensely Brilliant Lamp* (*dge
ldan bka' brgyud rin po che'i bka' srol phyag rgya chen po'i rtsa ba rgyas par
bshad pa yang gsal sgron me*), 12a.2–11b.2 in the Gangtok 1968 edition.

36 The reference here is to Hearers' and Solitary Realizers' practice as described in the Middle Way Consequence School, not to how their practice is described in the Hearer schools, these being the Great Exposition and Sūtra Schools.

37 The first entry in volume ga of his Collected Works.

38 For discussion of these increasingly subtle and more basic levels of consciousness, which are also experienced while dying, see earlier, p. 199, as well as His Holiness the Dalai Lama, *Mind of Clear Light: How to Live Well and Die Consciously,* 146-164, and Lati Rinbochay and Jeffrey Hopkins, *Death, Intermediate State, and Rebirth in Tibetan Buddhism,* 38-46.

39 See note 23.

40 Chapter I.29:

> The mental and physical aggregates arise
> From the conception of "I" which is false in fact.
> How could what is grown
> From a false seed be true?

See Jeffrey Hopkins, *Buddhist Advice for Living and Liberation: Nāgārjuna's Precious Garland* (Ithaca, N.Y.: Snow Lion Publications, 1998), 97.

41 The mother clear light is the mind of clear light of death itself; the child clear light is that manifested through cultivating the yogic path. An experienced yogi can utilize the mother clear light of death to realize the emptiness of inherent existence, this being called the meeting of the mother and child clear lights. See His Holiness the Dalai Lama, *Mind of Clear Light: How to Live Well and Die Consciously,* 164, and Lati Rinbochay and Jeffrey Hopkins, *Death, Intermediate State, and Rebirth in Tibetan Buddhism,* 47-48.

42 For discussion of empty forms, see the index entries in H.H. the Dalai Lama, Tenzin Gyatso, and Jeffrey Hopkins, *The Kālachakra Tantra: Rite of Initiation for the Stage of Generation* (London: Wisdom Publications, 1985; 2d rev. ed., 1989).

43 The Prāmāṇikas (Epistemologists) are primarily those following Dignāga and Dharmakīrti, the Sūtra School Following Reasoning, and the Mind-Only School Following Reasoning. They are called "Epistemologists" from their concern with valid cognition (*pramāṇa, tshad ma*), this being the source of their name.

44 In the sūtra systems paths are mainly consciousnesses which, when generated in the mental continuum, lead one to a higher state; however, right speech, which is form in some systems, is also considered a path.

Here in the Guhyasamāja system, the illusory body itself is considered to be the third of the five stages in the completion stage and thus is a path. In no sūtra system is the body itself considered to be a path.

45 In the system of the Sūtra Great Vehicle (called the Perfection Vehicle), it takes one period of a countless number of great eons for a Bodhisattva to overcome the innate afflictive obstructions—the habitual conception that phenomena inherently exist, as well as the other afflictive states that it induces. In Highest Yoga Tantra these are overcome in one instant of realizing emptiness with the very subtle mind of clear light, this being possible due to its tremendous force.

46 *lo gsum phyogs gsum;* a phase of the moon is one waxing or waning; thus, this is three years and one and a half months.

47 Leap-over refers to a mode of progress on the path that proceeds by way of the spontaneous, positive factors of the mind. See Khetsun Sangpo, *Tantric Practice in Nyingma,* trans. and ed. by Jeffrey Hopkins (London: Rider/Hutchinson, 1982; reprint, Ithaca, N.Y.: Snow Lion Publications, 1983), 182, 213, and 222.